T0356911

MICHELLE LANDER CAIN

NOT-YOUR-TYPICAL
Jelly Roll Quilts

14 Cute & Creative Projects

Make *the* Most *of* Your Precuts

C&T PUBLISHING
Another Maker Inspired!

Text copyright © 2025 by Michelle Lander Cain

Photography and artwork copyright © 2025 by C&T Publishing, Inc.

Publisher: Amy Barrett-Daffin

Creative Director: Gailen Runge

Senior Editor: Roxane Cerda

Editor: Gailen Runge

Technical Editor: Helen Frost

Cover/Book Designer: April Mostek

Production Coordinator: Tim Manibusan

Illustrator: Kirstie L. Petterson

Photography Coordinator: Rachel Ackley

Front cover photography by Melanie Zacek

Lifestyle photography by Melanie Zacek; instructional and subject photography by C&T Publishing, Inc., unless otherwise noted

Published by C&T Publishing, Inc., P.O. Box 1456, Lafayette, CA 94549

All rights reserved. No part of this work covered by the copyright hereon may be used in any form or reproduced by any means—graphic, electronic, or mechanical, including photocopying, recording, taping, or information storage and retrieval systems—without written permission from the publisher. The copyrights on individual artworks are retained by the artists as noted in *Not-Your-Typical Jelly Roll Quilts*. These designs may be used to make items for personal use only and may not be used for the purpose of personal profit. Items created to benefit nonprofit groups, or that will be publicly displayed, must be conspicuously labeled with the following credit: "Designs copyright © 2025 by Michelle Lander Cain from the book *Not-Your-Typical Jelly Roll Quilts* from C&T Publishing, Inc." Permission for all other purposes must be requested in writing from C&T Publishing, Inc.

Attention Copy Shops: Please note the following exception—publisher and author give permission to photocopy pages 110 and 111 for personal use only.

Attention Teachers: C&T Publishing, Inc., encourages the use of our books as texts for teaching. You can find lesson plans for many of our titles at ctpub.com or contact us at ctinfo@ctpub.com.

We take great care to ensure that the information included in our products is accurate and presented in good faith, but no warranty is provided, nor are results guaranteed. Having no control over the choices of materials or procedures used, neither the author nor C&T Publishing, Inc., shall have any liability to any person or entity with respect to any loss or damage caused directly or indirectly by the information contained in this book. For your convenience, we post an up-to-date listing of corrections on our website (ctpub.com). If a correction is not already noted, please contact our customer service department at ctinfo@ctpub.com or P.O. Box 1456, Lafayette, CA 94549.

Trademark (™) and registered trademark (®) names are used throughout this book. Rather than use the symbols with every occurrence of a trademark or registered trademark name, we are using the names only in the editorial fashion and to the benefit of the owner, with no intention of infringement.

Library of Congress Cataloging-in-Publication Data

Names: Cain, Michelle Lander, 1974- author.

Title: Not-your-typical Jelly Roll quilts : 14 cute & creative projects; make the most of your precuts / Michelle Lander Cain.

Description: Lafayette, CA : C&T Publishing, [2025] | Summary: "Not-Your-Typical Jelly Roll Quilts includes fourteen dynamic quilt projects using Jelly Rolls, from wall hangings and table runners to bed-size quilts. Take your Jelly Rolls to the next level with a variety of shapes, sizes, and blocks like rainbows, whales, cats, and more"--Provided by publisher.

Identifiers: LCCN 2024045477 | ISBN 9781644035542 (trade paperback) | ISBN 9781644035559 (ebook)

Subjects: LCSH: Quilting--Patterns.

Classification: LCC TT835 .C345 2025 | DDC 746.46/041--dc23/eng/20241128

LC record available at https://lccn.loc.gov/2024045477

Printed in China

10 9 8 7 6 5 4 3 2 1

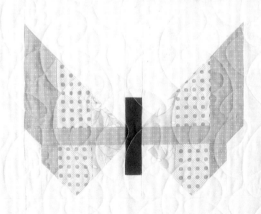

Dedication

This book is dedicated to Mom and Aunt Barbara, who put me on a crafty path years ago.

Acknowledgments

Many thanks to my supportive husband, Brad, and our two sons. They don't understand my obsession with quilting, but they know it feeds my soul as nothing else does and make space in our lives and our home for me to create.

I would not be the quilter I am today without the support and expertise I have found in the blogging community. For those of you who have been reading From Bolt to Beauty all these years, thank you!

I am also indebted to the members of the New Hampshire Modern Quilt Guild. They gave me a home as a new quilter and have taught me so much over the years. They are my people!

A special thank-you goes to Ophelia Chang, who not only longarmed the lion's share of the quilts in this collection, but who was also at the ready with advice or an encouraging word.

A big thank-you also goes to Gailen Runge, who saw the potential in my book idea and helped me bring it to fruition, and to Moda Fabrics and the Warm Company, whose generous donations helped me transform these designs into beautiful quilts.

And to friends old and new—Michelle Bartholomew, Cheryl Brickey, Megan Collins, Chelsea Folini, Sarah Fredette, Yvonne Fuchs, Laura Hennebury, Kim Soper—I love your big, beautiful quilty hearts.

CONTENTS

Introduction

AS A QUILTER, I LOVE JELLY ROLLS. It's how they display—all neatly wound together, with a peek of each fabric along the edge—that makes them so irresistible. They're the perfect fabric purchase because they offer a cross-section of a collection without taking up much space in my stash or much money out of my wallet.

As a quilt designer, I welcome the challenge of developing patterns for Jelly Rolls. Doing so works the part of my brain that enjoys a difficult crossword and does jigsaw puzzles without looking at the box top. For me, designing with Jelly Rolls is a quilty brainteaser!

Plus, those humble 2½-inch strips are more versatile than they seem, and I eagerly take on the task of writing new and creative patterns for them. The designs and instructions have to make sense for those long strips, though—simply cutting them into 2½-inch squares and sewing those squares into pretty quilt tops would be cheating. Instead, I cut my strips into long rectangles, half-hexies, and half-rectangle triangles and then sew them into rainbows, whales, giant stars, and medallion quilts. What results is a Jelly Roll pattern collection like no other.

The patterns here are great for quilters who consider themselves advanced beginners or above. There is no paper piecing, no partial seams or Y-seams—just traditionally pieced blocks and an occasional template. Still, some designs will come together faster than others. To gauge the complexity of a project in this book, look at how it rates on the spool scale from ▌to ▌▌▌. A ▌will prove to be pretty straightforward, but a ▌▌▌ will require more cutting and focus.

Are you ready to explore the creative possibilities of sewing with Jelly Rolls? I think these projects will surprise you!

JELLY ROLL BASICS

Many fabric manufacturers offer their own version of Jelly Rolls and have different names for these bundles. The strips always measure 2½ inches by the width of fabric, however, and are usually sold in groups of 40. The width of fabric can vary from one manufacturer to another, so for the patterns in this book, I've presumed there are at least 40 inches of usable fabric after removing the selvages. (The exception is *All the Xs*, which requires 41 inches.)

Because Moda Fabrics introduced the quilting world to Jelly Rolls back in 2006 and because, at heart, I am a Moda girl, I've sewn exclusively with Jelly Rolls from Moda designers for the projects in this book.

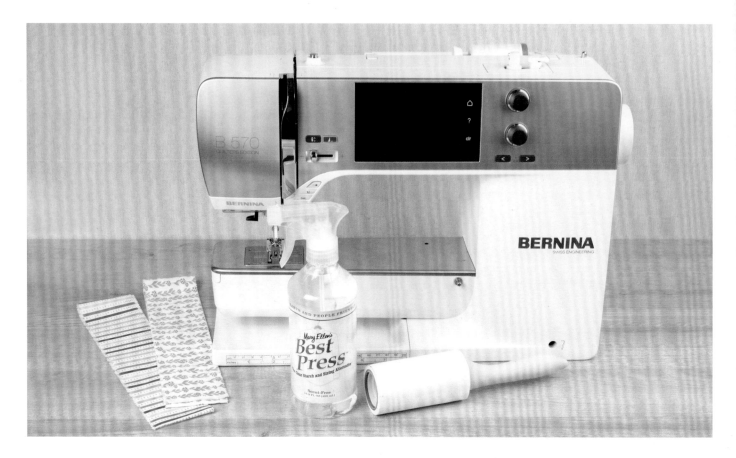

Assembling the Tools

In general, working with Jelly Rolls requires the standard sewing tools. You'll want your sewing machine in good working order, a sharp blade in your rotary cutter, and needles, pins, and thread at the ready.

Lint Roller

Moda Jelly Rolls, and comparable commercially produced 2½-inch strips, have pinked edges. Before opening up your spiral of strips, slide a sticky lint roller on both sides of the roll to corral any loose threads. Then keep the lint roller on hand for quick cleanups throughout the project.

Starch

Even if you usually forgo starching before cutting your fabric, give it a try with a Jelly Roll project here. There are a few designs that require cutting long rectangles. You may find in those cases that starch gives the strips extra body, enabling you to cut and sew more accurately. Other designs use small squares or blocks with bias edges, and starching the fabric can make handling those pieces easier.

To prepare Jelly Roll strips for starching, I lay them out on an old towel, spray them with starch, and let it absorb into the fabric. Then I transfer the strips in batches to my ironing board and press them without distorting the fabric's grain. I do the same for yardage.

Design Wall

Laying out a project on a design wall can help you envision your finished top before you sew it together. For most projects, a design wall is a nice-to-have tool. For those projects constructed as columns, like *Buoyant Hearts* (page 34) and *Myriad* (page 62), a design wall makes the process of determining fabric placement much easier.

A quick online search will produce a list of commercially made design walls, but you could use something as simple as a large piece of batting tacked temporarily up to a wall in your sewing space. The flannel backside of an outdoor vinyl tablecloth would work, too.

I bought two panels of foam board insulation at a home improvement store. I cut them down to 48 inches by 72 inches to make them more manageable to move around my house and covered them in batting. Sometimes I need just one to lay out a project; other times, I prop them up side by side. When I'm not using them, I can tuck them away behind a bookcase.

Measuring the Strips

Throughout the book, you will need to sew with a scant ¼-inch seam allowance. In other words, sew a seam that is a thread or two narrower than ¼ inch. But where do you measure that ¼ inch from on a Jelly Roll strip?

First, measure the width of the Jelly Roll strips you're using. The 2½ inches may measure from peak to peak or from valley to valley of the pinked edges. Where the 2½-inch mark falls will help you determine whether to sew a scant ¼ inch from the peak or the valley of your strips.

If your strips are a little bigger than 2½ inches, you could take the time to trim them down. To do so, fold them in half, matching one selvage end to the other, and use your ruler and rotary blade to remove the excess. Doing so is a matter of preference, though. I tend to avoid trimming my strips down—I find it easy to take too much off!

It's worth noting that I measure the strips of each Jelly Roll I use because I've found size discrepancies between rolls from the same manufacturer.

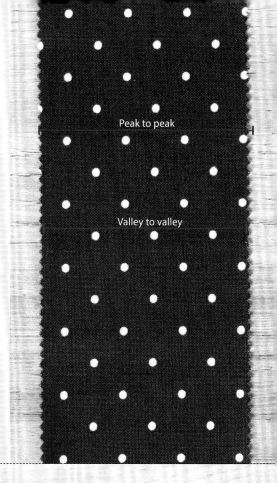

Peak to peak

Valley to valley

Supplementing a Jelly Roll

All the strips in a Jelly Roll may not work for the project you have in mind. Some prints might not provide enough contrast with your background fabric. Others may have a strong directionality or geometry that might not work well with the pattern at hand. And some patterns will require more of a particular color than you'll find in one Jelly Roll. (Consider *Lucky Medallion*, page 80. You want all your four-leaf clovers to be green!) Don't presume you have to buy a second roll to solve the problem, though. If you don't have enough of the required strips, you can easily supplement with other fabric.

Fat quarters and regular ¼-yard selvage-to-selvage cuts are the best options for adding to your Jelly Roll. A 2½-inch cut from a ¼ yard is equal to a Jelly Roll strip and leaves you 6½ inches for future projects. Fat quarters typically measure 18 inches by 20 inches. Two cuts 2½ inches by 20 inches equal a Jelly Roll strip. Often, determining the number of cuts required from fat quarters is as simple as multiplying the number of Jelly Roll strips by two. Other times, and depending on how a particular pattern cuts the strips, you may need more than two fat quarter cuts to provide the necessary pieces.

1 cut 2½″ × 40″ = a Jelly Roll strip

2 cuts 2½″ × 20″ = a Jelly Roll strip

Solids and Blenders

An easy solution to adding to your Jelly Roll is to use solids and blenders from your stash. If you don't have ¼-yard cuts or fat quarters on hand, a handful of scraps at least 2½ inches wide may do the job.

Other Collections from the Same Designer

I also like to scour my stash for other fabrics from the designer of the Jelly Roll I'm working with. Some designers have a signature palette or use colors that coordinate well between collections. With *Lucky Medallion* (page 80), I supplemented greens from Vanessa Goertzen's Country Rose line with greens from her Folktale collection. The colors are different but still play well together, and the variety adds interest to the circle of four-leaf clovers.

Fabrics in Multiple Colorways

A great way to re-create the matchy-matchy feel of a fabric collection is to use one print in two colorways, a technique I used with *Step Dance* (page 56). To flesh out the yellow colorway of the Sweetwater Jelly Roll I was using, I added a yellow floral from Basic Grey to the mix. I had plenty of Sweetwater strips in blue but included the same Basic Grey floral in blue, too, just to create the impression that the Basic Grey fabrics belonged with the Sweetwater prints.

Things to Consider

When supplementing a Jelly Roll, I think it's important to consider genre: Does the collection have a vintage vibe? Is it more modern, or does it feature novelty prints? You want to maintain the look and feel of the Jelly Roll with any additions.

If you decide you need to buy fabric to add to your Jelly Roll, start with your local quilt shop. Online fabric retailers often require a minimum cut, and there's no reason to buy ½ yard when you need just a 2½-inch cut or two. Plus, you'll be able to match any new additions better in person than you will on a computer.

And of course, if you want to get started today and don't have a Jelly Roll on hand—or if you delight in the process of assembling a fabric pull—you can always design your own. Raid your stash of yardage and fat quarters to cut and compile a collection of strips that is uniquely you.

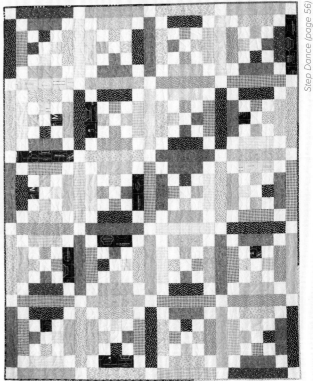

Step Dance (page 56)

Putting Leftover Strips to Good Use

After a Jelly Roll project or two, you will start to accumulate leftover strips. I have a big bin of scrappy 2½-inch squares, so I am always tempted to cut those strips into squares and call it a day. There are plenty of ways, however, to use up those scraps other than relegating them to the scrap bin.

Projects for a Few Strips

This book begins with a handful of small projects. Take stock of your leftover strips and scraps—you may have enough on hand to create *Five Little Ghosts* (page 20) or *Neighborly* (page 16). You could also sew *Pod Patrol* (page 42) with just 10 Jelly Roll strips for the whales and the optional single-fabric waves.

Neighborly (page 16)

A Low-Volume Option

Meow Mates (page 50) is especially suited for leftover low-volume strips. I incorporated low-volume prints from the Jelly Rolls I used throughout this book in my version of the quilt.

A Quilt for Many Strips

Pixelated Herringbone (page 74) is another quilt that would work well with scraps from different collections. My version uses a light and a dark aqua to rein in the brilliant colors of Melody Miller's Stay Gold collection. A scrappy version could rely on, say, two shades of gray to edge the squares from multiple fabric lines.

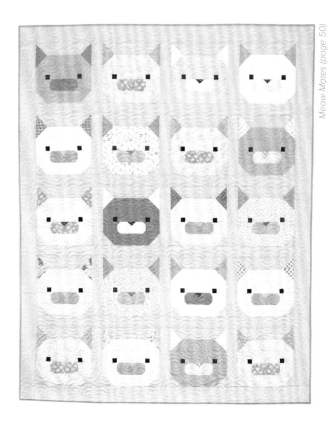

Meow Mates (page 50)

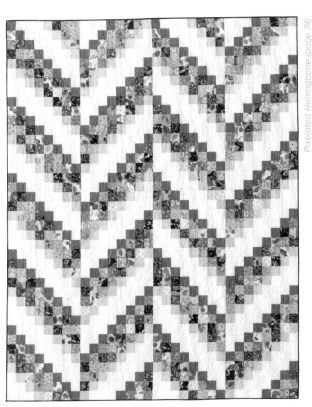

Pixelated Herringbone (page 74)

Scrappy Bindings and Backings

Bindings and backings are other opportunities to use leftover scraps. Sew together Jelly Roll strips for the perfectly scrappy binding, as I did for *Step Dance* (page 56).

You could also turn your scraps into a design on the back of your quilt. For projects like *I Heart Rainbows* (page 90) or *Butterfly Season* (page 96), make a few extra blocks and place them on the back.

I almost always use backings as a venue for scraps, even when I'm not working with Jelly Rolls. Not only does this approach allow me to put my scraps to good use, but it also reduces the amount of yardage I need to purchase for backings. My basic formula is this: (1) Buy enough yardage to accommodate the length a project requires. (2) Remove the selvages, and cut the fabric lengthwise (I think it's easier to make this cut purposefully off-center; 15 inches from one edge is a good spot). (3) Add enough scraps to that center space to achieve the required width. (4) Sew the scrappy center to the sides.

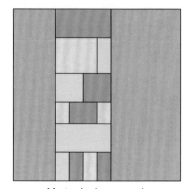

My typical approach to pieced backings

I followed that recipe for *Tag Sale Floral*'s backing. I took a 1½-yard cut of fabric for the back and filled the center with Jelly Roll scraps that I cut into rectangles 2½ inches by 8½ inches and then sewed into sets of four.

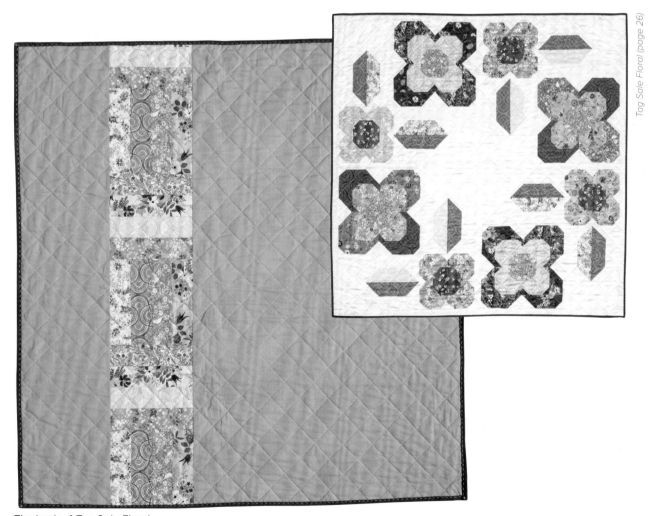

Tag Sale Floral (page 26)

The back of *Tag Sale Floral*

Tackling Some Basic Techniques

There are a few techniques to discuss before you embark on these Jelly Roll patterns: pressing, sewing half-square triangles, snowballing corners, working with strip sets, and taking a victory lap.

Pressing

In general, I like to press my seams open. I think open seams make for a flatter, easier-to-quilt top, especially if I end up quilting it myself on my domestic. So, throughout the book, most patterns instruct you to press the seams open.

The exception is when pressing to the side allows me to nest seams and save time by sewing accurately without pinning. *Pixelated Herringbone* (page 74) and *Pod Patrol* (page 42) are great opportunities to use this approach.

Quilters tend to be very opinionated about pressing. If you'd prefer to press seams to the side when the instructions indicate to press open, go for it. Just know that pressing those spots to one side will not facilitate nesting.

When I press, I first lay my iron on the seam flat, without opening up the fabric. Doing so is often called "setting the seam." I take this extra step because I think it makes the seam more malleable and creates a flatter press. After setting the seam, I then open up the sewn unit and press the seam either open or to one side.

Sewing Half-Square Triangles

In this book, the half-square triangles (HSTs) are made one at a time. To make a HST, draw a diagonal line from one corner to another on the wrong side of a 2½-inch square. Place that on top of another 2½-inch square. Sew directly on the line, trim ¼ inch from the seam on one side, and press the seam open. These instructions create a 2½-inch unfinished HST (2-inch finished HST) that does not require trimming.

Pod Patrol (page 42)

Snowballing Corners

The technique of snowballing corners is comparable to creating HSTs, except the two pieces of fabric are different sizes. To snowball a corner, draw a diagonal line from one corner to another on the wrong side of a square of fabric, whatever size the pattern calls for. Place it on top of the larger piece of fabric. Sew directly on the line, trim ¼ inch from the seam, and press the seam open.

I use a Clover Hera Marker to mark my diagonal lines. As long as the lighting in my sewing space is good, I can follow the line without a problem. If the square is 2½ inches or smaller, though, I get good results (and save a little time) by folding the piece in half diagonally and finger pressing the line instead of marking it.

Working with Strip Sets

Some patterns in this book, such as *Myriad* (page 62) and *All the Xs* (page 102), require sewing long strips together and then cutting those strip sets into smaller units. It's an effective strategy for cutting and piecing more quickly.

Sewing long strips, however, can cause bowing. To minimize this problem, use a short stitch length of about 1.7mm, or 14 to 15 stitches per inch. And when you're sewing multiple strips together, alternate the direction you sew from one strip to the next. For example, consider the situation depicted in the figure below. The first two strips were sewn from top to bottom. When adding a third strip to the set, sew it from bottom to top.

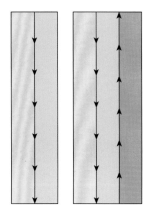

When it comes to cutting those strips into smaller units, line up the marks on your ruler with the seams, not with the edges of the strip set. You'll cut your pieces more accurately that way.

Also, if the width of the fabric you're using permits, cut your strips a little longer than what a pattern requires. For example, if you're cutting Jelly Roll strips in half and can get 20½ inches instead of just 20 inches out of each strip, take that extra ½ inch. This wiggle room will allow you to square up the set periodically as you cut units from it.

Taking a Victory Lap

Some of the patterns in this book, such as *Buoyant Hearts* (page 34) and *Pixelated Herringbone* (page 74), create a lot of seams along the perimeter of the quit top. To keep these seams secure while handling and quilting the top, take a "victory lap" before basting. In other words, stay-stitch the top by sewing ⅛ inch from the edge. That line of stitches will take a few extra minutes, but it serves a good purpose and will end up under the binding and away from view.

A Few Words Before Beginning

As with any pattern, please read the one you want to make from this collection in its entirety before you cut anything. Also, the fabric requirements for the background and any accent yardage include some overage to accommodate squaring up the fabric and making a cutting error or two. (The bigger quilts include more overage than the smaller ones.) Finally, I know it can be hard to take the time to sew a test block when you're eager to start a new project, but your future self will appreciate it!

Buoyant Hearts (page 34)

Neighborly

FINISHED BLOCK SIZE: 10″ × 10″ ✦ **FINISHED QUILT SIZE: 30½″ × 30½″**

Neighborly is perfect for scraps—so gather your Jelly Roll scraps, or slice your scrap bin into 2½-inch strips. Either way, this pattern is a quick sew!

Fabric Requirements

Instructions presume at least a 40″ width of fabric (WOF) after removing the selvages. The 13 Jelly Roll strips will provide some variety in each of the blocks (and will produce some scraps). For added interest, cut the pieces specified in the Cutting section from a greater number of prints.

- At least 13 Jelly Roll strips
    3 each in rust, blue, and beige (or in 3 colorways of your choice)
    4 in green (or in the colorway of your choice)
- 1 yard background fabric
- 1⅛ yards backing*
- 39″ × 39″ batting*
- 2 squares 5″ × 5″ for hanging**
- ⅜ yard binding

> ** The backing and batting requirements include 8″ of overhang to accommodate longarming services. Sewists who plan on quilting this project on a domestic machine may choose to piece a smaller backing (and use less batting) than the 39″ × 39″ size called for in the pattern.*
>
> *** For details on hanging* Neighborly*, see Preparing to Hang a Project (page 109).*

Cutting

JELLY ROLL STRIPS

Rust Colorway

From 3 strips, cut a total of:
    3 rectangles 2½″ × 10½″
    4 rectangles 2½″ × 6½″
    2 rectangles 2½″ × 6″

Blue Colorway

From 3 strips, cut a total of:
    6 rectangles 2½″ × 10½″
    4 rectangles 2½″ × 6″

Beige Colorway

From 3 strips, cut a total of:
    8 rectangles 2½″ × 6½″

Green Colorway

From 4 strips, cut a total of:
    3 rectangles 2½″ × 10½″
    8 rectangles 2½″ × 6½″
    2 rectangles 2½″ × 6″

BACKGROUND

Cut 1 strip 6½″ × WOF.
    Subcut into 4 rectangles 6½″ × 9½″.
Cut 1 strip 3½″ × WOF.
    Subcut into 10 squares 3½″ × 3½″.
Cut 4 strips 2½″ × WOF.*
    Subcut into 10 rectangles 2½″ × 10½″ (each strip can yield 3).
    > ** Note: If the usable fabric after removing selvages is at least 42″, cut just 3 strips (each strip can yield 4).*
Cut 2 strips 1½″ × WOF.
    Subcut into 10 rectangles 1½″ × 6½″ (each strip can yield 6).

BINDING

Cut 4 strips 2½″ × WOF.

Pieced and quilted
by Michelle Cain

Social media:
#NeighborlyQuilt

*FABRICS USED
Jelly Roll: Flower Pot by
Lella Boutique for Moda
Background fabric: Moda Bella
Solids in Off-White*

Construction

All seams are a scant ¼″ unless otherwise indicated. Press the seams open. For more specifics on snowballing, see Snowballing Corners (page 14).

Sew the Striped House Blocks

1 Gather the 4 rust rectangles 2½″ × 6½″.

2 Sew the rectangles together along the long edges to make a unit 6½″ × 8½″. Press.

3 Snowball a top corner of the unit with a background square 3½″ × 3½″ as indicated in the figure. Trim and press.

4 Snowball the other top corner of the unit with a background square 3½″ × 3½″ as indicated in the figure. Trim and press.

5 Sew a background rectangle 1½″ × 6½″ onto the top and bottom of the unit. Press.

6 Sew a background rectangle 2½″ × 10½″ onto each side of the unit. Press.

7 Repeat Steps 1–6 with 2 sets of 4 beige rectangles 2½″ × 6½″ and 2 sets of 4 green rectangles 2½″ × 6½″. In total, there will be 5 Striped House blocks.

Sew the Striped Background Blocks

The pieces for the Striped Background blocks require some further cutting before sewing.

1 Gather these pieces in the blue colorway: 3 rectangles 2½″ × 10½″ and 2 rectangles 2½″ × 6″.

2 Cut 1 rectangle 2½″ × 10½″ into 2 middle rectangles 2½″ × 4½″ and 1 middle rectangle 2½″ × 1½″. Set the other 2 rectangles 2½″ × 10½″ to the side.

3 Cut 1 rectangle 2½″ × 6″ into 1 side A rectangle 2½″ × 4½″ and 1 side A rectangle 2½″ × 1½″.

4 Cut the remaining rectangle 2½″ × 6″ into 1 side B rectangle 2½″ × 4½″ and 1 side B rectangle 2½″ × 1½″.

5 Sew 1 middle rectangle 2½″ × 4½″ to the side A rectangle 2½″ × 4½″ along the long edges. Press. Sew the remaining middle rectangle 2½″ × 4½″ to the side B rectangle 2½″ × 4½″ along the long edges. Press. Both units will be 4½″ × 4½″ (unfinished).

6 Snowball a top corner of a background rectangle 6½″ × 9½″ with a square from Step 5 as indicated in the figure. Trim and press.

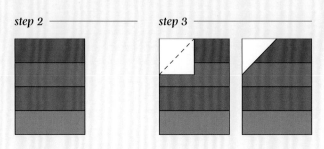

step 2 ———— step 3 ————

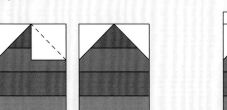 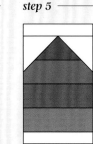

step 4 ———— step 5 ————

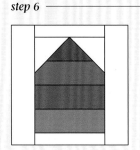

step 6 ————————————————

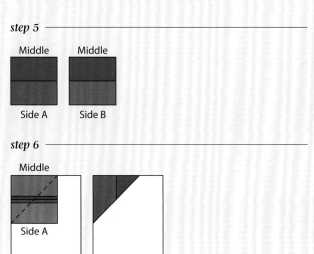

Sew the Striped Background Blocks

step 5 ————

Middle Middle

Side A   Side B

step 6 ————

Middle

Side A

7 Snowball the other top corner of the background rectangle with a square from Step 5 as indicated in the figure. Trim and press.

8 Sew the 3 rectangles 2½″ × 1½″ together along the short edges in the order they appear on the unit from Step 7. Press.

9 Sew the unit from Step 8 onto the bottom of the unit from Step 7. Press.

10 Sew the 2 rectangles 2½″ × 10½″ to either side of the unit. Press.

11 Repeat Steps 1–10 with another set of blue pieces, 1 set of rust pieces, and 1 set of green pieces. In total, there will be 4 Striped Background blocks.

Assemble the Top

1 Following the Quilt Assembly Diagram, lay out the 9 blocks.

2 Sew the blocks into 3 rows. Press.

3 Sew the 3 rows together. Press.

Finishing the Wall Hanging

For more details on completing a quilt, including how to prepare a quilt for hanging, see Finishing the Projects (page 108). See the note under Fabric Requirements (page 16) about the backing and batting.

1 Trim 1⅛ yards backing fabric to approximately 39″ × 39″.

2 Build the quilt sandwich: backing + batting + quilt top. Baste.

3 Quilt as desired.

4 If adding hanging triangles to the back of the quilt (see Preparing to Hang a Project, page 109), baste them to the top corners.

5 Sew the 4 binding strips 2½″ × WOF together, end to end, with a diagonal seam. Bind and enjoy your finished wall hanging!

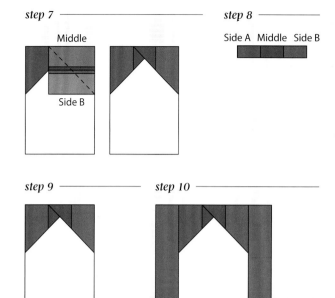

step 7 — Middle — Side B
step 8 — Side A Middle Side B
step 9 — *step 10*

Assemble the Top

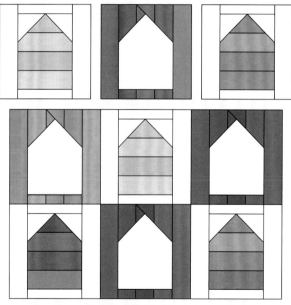

Quilt Assembly Diagram

Five Little Ghosts

FINISHED BLOCK SIZE: 8½″ × 10¾″ ✦ **FINISHED QUILT SIZE: 49″ × 16½″**

These ghosts are more sweet than spooky, and because each requires a single Jelly Roll strip, they're easy to sew with leftover low-volume fabrics from other projects.

Fabric Requirements

Instructions presume at least a 40″ width of fabric (WOF) after removing the selvages.

- 5 Jelly Roll strips for the ghosts
- ⅛ yard or scrap of black fabric for the eyes and mouths
- ⅞ yard background fabric*
- 1½ yards backing**
- 57″ × 25″ batting**
- ⅜ yard binding

> ** These instructions presume the background fabric is a solid or nondirectional fabric. (The sample was sewn with a directional print, and the background pieces were cut to maintain that orientation.)*
>
> *** The backing and batting requirements include 8″ of overhang to accommodate longarming services. Sewists who plan on quilting this project on a domestic machine may choose to piece a smaller backing (and use less batting) than the 57″ × 25″ size called for in the pattern.*

Cutting

JELLY ROLL STRIPS

From each of 5 Jelly Roll strips, cut:
   1 A rectangle 2½″ × 5¼″
   1 B rectangle 2½″ × 4¼″
Trim the remnants down to 2¼″ × the remaining WOF, and cut from each:
   2 C rectangles 2¼″ × 2¾″
   2 D rectangles 2¼″ × 2″
   2 E rectangles 2¼″ × 1″
Trim the remnants down to 2″ × the remaining WOF, and cut from each:
   2 F rectangles 2″ × 8″
   2 G rectangles 2″ × 1¼″

BLACK FABRIC (EYES/MOUTHS)

Cut 1 strip 2¼″ × WOF.
   Subcut into 5 mouth rectangles 2¼″ × 1½″.
   Trim the remnant down to 2″ × the remaining WOF, and subcut 10 eye rectangles 2″ × 1¼″.

BACKGROUND FABRIC

Blocks

Reserve the background scraps.

Cut 2 strips 3¾″ × WOF.
   Subcut into 5 rectangles 3¾″ × 9″ (each strip can yield 4).
Cut 4 strips 2¼″ × WOF.
   Subcut 1 strip into 8 rectangles 2¼″ × 5″.
   Subcut 1 strip into 8 rectangles 2¼″ × 4½″.
   Subcut 1 strip into 2 rectangles 2¼″ × 5″ and 2 rectangles 2¼″ × 4½″.
   Subcut 1 strip into 10 squares 2¼″ × 2¼″.
From the scraps, cut:
   15 squares 1½″ × 1½″
   10 squares 1¼″ × 1¼″
   5 rectangles 2½″ × 1″

Sashing and Borders

Cut 5 strips 1½″ × WOF.

BINDING

Cut 4 strips 2½″ × WOF.

Pieced and quilted
by Michelle Cain

Social media:
#FiveLittleGhostsQuilt

FABRICS USED
Jelly Roll: White-on-white prints
from various fabric collections
Background fabric: Spooky Darlings
from Ruby Star Society

Construction

All seams are a scant ¼" unless otherwise indicated. Press seams open. For more specifics on snowballing, see Snowballing Corners (page 14).

Sew the Arm Units

1 Snowball a C rectangle with a background square 2¼" × 2¼" as indicated in the figure. Trim and press. This is a left arm.

2 Snowball a C rectangle with a background square 2¼" × 2¼" as indicated in the figure. Trim and press. This is a right arm.

3 Repeat Steps 1–2 to make a total of 5 left arm units and 5 right arm units.

Sew the Head Units

1 Snowball a D rectangle with a background square 1½" × 1½" as indicated in the figure. Trim and press. This is the left side of a head.

2 Snowball a D rectangle with a background square 1½" × 1½" as indicated in the figure. Trim and press. This is the right side of a head.

3 Repeat Steps 1–2 to make a total of 5 left sides and 5 right sides.

Sew the Mouth Units

1 Sew an E rectangle on both long sides of a mouth rectangle. Press.

2 Repeat to make a total of 5 mouth/E units.

Sew the Eye Units

1 Sew an eye rectangle to a G rectangle. Press.

2 Repeat to make a total of 10 eye/G units.

Sew the Arm Units

step 1

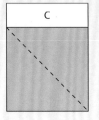 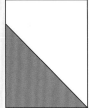

step 2

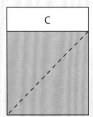 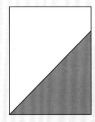

Sew the Head Units

step 1

step 2

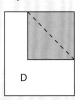 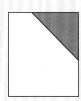

Sew the Mouth Units

step 1

Sew the Eye Units

step 1

Snowball the Body Segments

1 Snowball the bottom left corner of an F rectangle with a background square 1¼″ × 1¼″.

2 Snowball the bottom left corner of an A rectangle with a background square 1¼″ × 1¼″.

3 Snowball the bottom left corner of an F rectangle with a background square 1½″ × 1½″.

4 Repeat Steps 1–3 to make 5 of each body segment configuration.

Complete the Ghost Blocks

1 Lay out the pieces for 1 Ghost block as indicated in the figure.

2 Sew the pieces into 5 columns. Press.

3 Sew the 5 columns into a complete block, measuring 9″ × 11¼″ (unfinished). Press.

4 Repeat Steps 1–3 to make a total of 5 Ghost blocks.

Snowball the Body Segments

steps 1–3

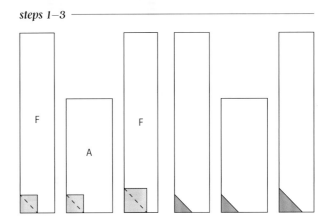

Complete the Ghost Blocks

step 1

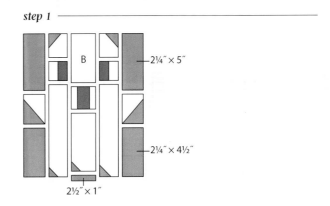

Assemble the Top

Refer to the Quilt Assembly Diagram for illustrations of the steps that follow.

ADD BACKGROUND BLOCKS

1 Sew a background rectangle 3¾″ × 9″ on the top of 3 Ghost blocks. Press.

2 Sew a background rectangle 3¾″ × 9″ on the bottom of the remaining 2 Ghost blocks. Press.

SEW THE SASHING AND BORDERS

1 Sew the 5 sashing/border strips 1½″ × WOF together, end to end. Press the seams.

2 From the resulting long strip, cut 6 vertical sashing rectangles 1½″ × 14½″. Set the rest aside.

3 Sew 4 vertical sashing rectangles in between the 5 Ghost blocks to create 1 row. Press.

4 Sew the remaining 2 vertical sashing rectangles to either end of the row. Press.

5 Measure the runner top at 3 points (the top, bottom, and middle) to find the average length. (It should be about 49″.)

6 Cut 2 strips that length from the remaining long 1½″ strip. Sew those strips on the top and bottom of the runner. Press.

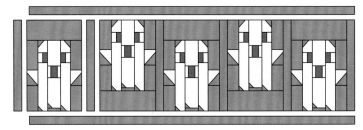

Quilt Assembly Diagram

Finishing the Runner

For more details on completing a quilt, see Finishing the Projects (page 108). See the note under Fabric Requirements (page 20) about the backing and batting.

1 To make the backing, cut the 1½ yards backing fabric into 2 strips 25″ × WOF. Using a ½″ seam allowance, sew the 2 strips together along the short edges. Press the seam open. Trim to approximately 57″ × 25″.

2 Build the quilt sandwich: backing + batting + quilt top. Baste.

3 Quilt as desired.

4 Sew the 4 binding strips 2½″ × WOF together, end to end, with a diagonal seam. Bind and enjoy your finished runner!

EMBROIDERING THE DETAILS

After quilting this project, I embellished my ghosts with some embroidery. This simple technique took just a few minutes and brought the ghouls' silly personalities to life.

To do the same after quilting and binding your project, follow these steps:

1 Gather together a hand needle and thread. I used a 12-weight Aurifil thread, but you'll get equally good results with other options, such as an 8-weight thread or multiple strands of embroidery floss.

2 Cut 12 inches or so of thread, double-knot one end, and thread your needle.

3 Insert the needle from the right side of the project, about an inch from where you want your first cross-stitch to appear. Pull the knot through the quilt top only, burying it between the top and the batting.

4 To make the first arm of the cross-stitch, bring the needle up through Point A and down through the quilt top, about ¼ inch away, at Point B.

5 Do not bring the needle through the back of the project. Instead, travel inside the quilt to bring the needle up again at Point C. (Be careful when traveling under low-volume fabrics, though. You don't want dark thread to be visible through light fabrics.)

6 To finish the second arm of the cross-stitch, take the needle down at Point D. Again, do not bring the needle through to the back of the project. Travel inside the quilt to the point at which you want to start your second cross-stitch.

7 When you're making your last cross-stitch, stop after bringing your needle up through Point C. Make a knot in the thread a little more than ¼ inch away from that spot. Take the needle down through Point D, pull the knot into the interior of the quilt, and bring the needle up through the top about an inch from Point D. Trim the thread close to the quilt top.

Tag Sale Floral

Skill Level

FINISHED BLOCK SIZE: 20″ × 20″ ✦ **FINISHED QUILT SIZE: 43½″ × 43½″**

When I designed *Tag Sale Floral*, I envisioned its flowers encircling items on my kitchen table, but the size is perfect for a wall hanging, too.

Fabric Requirements

Instructions presume at least a 40″ width of fabric (WOF) after removing the selvages.

- 22 Jelly Roll strips
    - 2 for the flower centers
    - 8 for the small flowers
    - 8 for the large petals
    - 4 for the leaves
- 1⅝ yards background fabric
- 3 yards backing*
- 52″ × 52″ batting
- ½ yard binding

    * See Scrappy Bindings and Backings (page 12) to learn how to sew this backing with just 1½ yards.

Cutting

JELLY ROLL STRIPS

Keep the pieces cut from 1 Jelly Roll strip together.

Flower Centers

Cut 2 Jelly Roll strips in half to make 4 flower center strips 2½″ × 20+″.

Small Flowers

From each of 8 Jelly Roll strips, cut:
- 4 rectangles 2½″ × 4½″
- 4 squares 2½″ × 2½″
- 4 squares 1½″ × 1½″

Large Petals

From each of 8 Jelly Roll strips, cut:
- 2 rectangles 2½″ × 6½″
- 2 rectangles 2½″ × 4½″
- 6 squares 1½″ × 1½″

Leaves

Cut 4 Jelly Roll strips in half to make 8 leaf strips 2½″ × 20+″.

BACKGROUND FABRIC

Blocks

Cut 2 strips 8½″ × WOF.
   Subcut 1 strip into 8 rectangles 8½″ × 4½″.
   Subcut 1 strip into 16 rectangles 8½″ × 2½″.
Cut 4 strips 2½″ × WOF.
   Subcut into 64 squares 2½″ × 2½″ (each strip can yield 16).
Cut 3 strips 1½″ × WOF.
   Subcut into 64 squares 1½″ × 1½″ (each strip can yield 26).

Sashing and Borders

Cut 7 strips 1½″ × WOF.

BINDING

Cut 5 strips 2½″ × WOF.

Pieced by
Michelle Cain

Quilted by
Ophelia Chang

Social media:
#TagSaleFloralQuilt

FABRICS USED
Jelly Roll: Lady Bird by
Crystal Manning for Moda
Background fabric: Moda
Bella Solids in Porcelain

Construction

All seams are a scant ¼″ unless otherwise indicated. Press the seams open. For more specifics on snowballing, see Snowballing Corners (page 14).

Sew the Flower Centers

1 Gather 2 flower center strips 2½″ × 20″ in the same print. Sew them together along the long edges. Press.

2 Repeat with the remaining 2 flower center strips, for a total of 2 strip sets.

3 Cut the 2 sets into 8 flower centers 4½″ × 4½″ (each set can yield 4). Discard the scraps.

Determine the Fabric Combinations

1 Group each flower center with the pieces for a small flower *in the same print*: 4 rectangles 2½″ × 4½″, 4 squares 2½″ × 2½″, and 4 squares 1½″ × 1½″. There will be 8 groups.

2 To each of 4 groups, add 12 background squares 1½″ × 1½″. These are groups 1–4.

3 To each of the remaining 4 groups, add the large petal pieces *in each of 2 different prints*: 2 rectangles 2½″ × 6½″, 2 rectangles 2½″ × 4½″, and 6 squares 1½″ × 1½″. Also add to each group 8 background squares 2½″ × 2½″ and 4 background squares 1½″ × 1½″. These are groups 5–8.

Sew the Small Flowers

For the steps that follow, use groups 1–4, sewing 1 group at a time.

1 Snowball the 4 corners of the flower center with 4 small flower squares 1½″ × 1½″. Trim and press.

2 Snowball 2 corners on the long side of the 4 small flower rectangles with 2 background squares 1½″ × 1½″. Trim and press.

3 Sew 2 units from Step 2 together along the short edges. Press, and repeat with the remaining 2 units from Step 2.

4 Snowball 1 corner of the 4 small flower squares 2½″ × 2½″ with 1 background square 1½″ × 1½″ as indicated in the figure. Trim and press.

Sew the Flower Centers

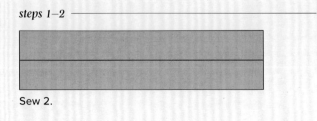

steps 1–2

Sew 2.

step 3

Cut 8.

Sew the Small Flowers

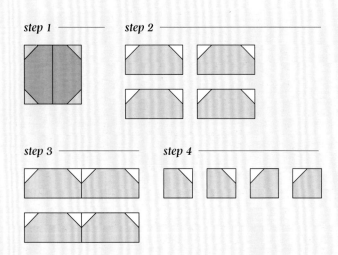

step 1   *step 2*

step 3   *step 4*

5 Sew 2 units from Step 4 together, matching the snowballed edges. Press, and repeat with the remaining 2 units from Step 4.

6 Sew the units from Step 5 to either side of the flower center from Step 1 as indicated in the figure.

7 Lay out the 3 rows and sew them together. Press.

8 Repeat Steps 1–7 for the remaining 3 Small Flowers.

Sew the Large Flowers

For the steps that follow, use groups 5–8, sewing 1 group at a time.

1 Snowball the 4 corners of the flower center with 4 small flower squares 1½″ × 1½″. Trim and press.

2 Snowball 2 corners on the long side of the 4 small flower rectangles with 2 large petal squares 1½″ × 1½″ in the same print. Trim and press.

3 Sew 2 units from Step 2 together along the short edges as indicated in the figure. Press, and repeat with the remaining 2 units from Step 2. (Note the placement of the fabric in the snowballed corners: This step produces 2 identical units.)

4 Snowball 1 corner of the 4 small flower squares 2½″ × 2½″ with 1 large petal square 1½″ × 1½″ as indicated in the figure. Trim and press.

5 Sew 2 units from Step 4 together as indicated in the figure. Press, and repeat with the remaining 2 units from Step 4. (The fabric placement in the unit from Step 3 determines the placement here: The print from the left side of Step 3 appears on the right here. The print from the right side of Step 3 appears on the left here.)

6 Sew the units from Step 5 to either side of the flower center from Step 1 as indicated in the figure.

7 Lay out the 3 rows and sew them together. Press.

8 Lay out the large petal rectangles around the unit from Step 7, matching adjacent prints, as indicated in the Large Flower Assembly Diagram (page 30). Snowball the large petal rectangles 2½″ × 4½″ with background squares 2½″ × 2½″ as indicated in step 8 figure. Trim and press.

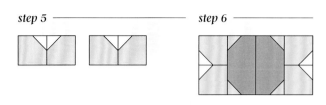

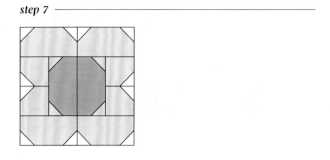

Sew the Large Flowers

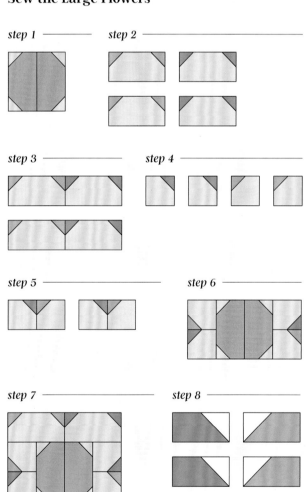

9 Snowball the large petal rectangles 2½″ × 6½″ with background squares 2½″ × 2½″ and 1½″ × 1½″ as indicated in the step 9 figure. Trim and press.

10 Sew the snowballed large petal rectangles 2½″ × 6½″ together along the short edges. Press. Sew the snowballed large petal rectangles 2½″ × 4½″ together along the short edges. Press.

11 Sew the units made of 2½″ × 4½″ rectangles to the small flower as indicated in the diagram. Press.

12 Sew the 3 rows together. Press.

13 Repeat Steps 1–12 for the remaining 3 Large Flowers.

Sew the Leaves

1 Gather 2 leaf strips 2½″ × 20″ in the same print or in different prints, as shown in the sample. Sew them together along the long edges. Press.

2 Repeat with the remaining 6 leaf strips, for a total of 4 strip sets.

3 Cut the 4 sets into 8 leaf rectangles 4½″ × 8½″ (each set can yield 2). Discard the scraps.

4 Snowball each leaf rectangle with 4 background squares 2½″ × 2½″ as indicated in the figure. Trim and press.

5 Sew background rectangles 2½″ × 8½″ to both long sides of each leaf. Press.

6 Sew a background rectangle 8½″ × 4½″ to an end of each leaf as indicated in the figure. Press.

✣ **Tip** ✣

The rectangle added in Step 6 will determine a leaf's orientation in the finished block. To plan the orientation of the leaves in advance, look ahead to the Quilt Assembly Diagram.

---

step 9

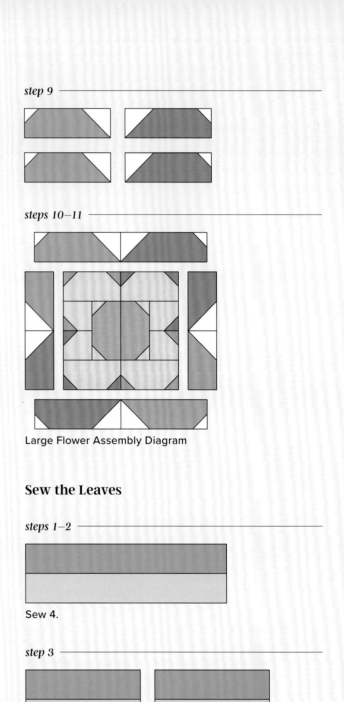

steps 10–11

Large Flower Assembly Diagram

Sew the Leaves

steps 1–2

Sew 4.

step 3

Cut 8.

step 4　　　　step 5

step 6

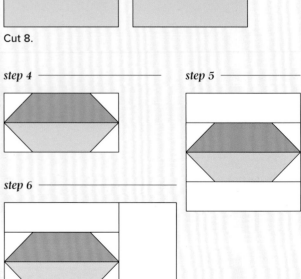

Complete the Blocks

1 Lay out a block as indicated in the figure.

2 Sew the pieces into 2 rows. Press.

3 Sew the rows together. Press.

4 Repeat Steps 1–3 to make a total of 4 blocks.

Assemble the Top

Refer to the Quilt Assembly Diagram for illustrations of the steps that follow.

1 Lay out the completed blocks, rotating the blocks when necessary.

2 Sew the 7 sashing/border strips 1½″ × WOF together, end to end. Press the seams.

3 From the resulting long strip, cut 2 vertical sashing rectangles 1½″ × 20½″. Set the rest aside.

4 Sew the vertical sashing rectangles in between 2 blocks to create 2 rows. Press.

5 Measure each row, and calculate the average length. (It should be about 41½″.)

6 Cut 3 horizontal sashing strips that length from the strip set aside in Step 3.

7 Sew the horizontal sashing strips in between the 2 rows and at the top and bottom of the quilt top. Press.

8 Measure the quilt top at 3 points (each side and the middle) to find the average length. (It should be about 43½″.)

9 Cut 2 strips that length from the remaining 1½″ strip. Sew those strips on the sides of the quilt top. Press.

Complete the Blocks

step 1

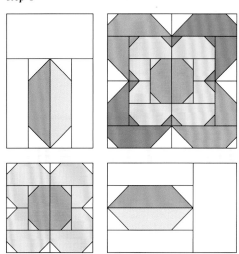

Assemble the Top

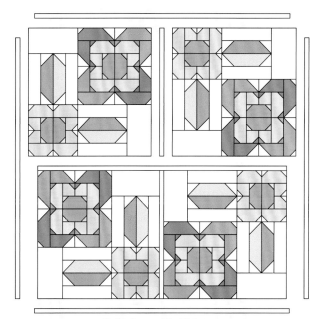

Quilt Assembly Diagram

Finishing the Table Topper

For more details on completing a quilt, see Finishing the Projects (page 108). For an alternative approach to piecing this backing, see Scrappy Bindings and Backings (page 12).

1 To make the backing, cut the 3 yards of backing fabric into 2 strips 52″ × WOF. Using a ½″ seam allowance, sew the 2 strips together along the long edges. Press the seam open. Trim to approximately 52″ × 52″.

2 Build the quilt sandwich: backing + batting + quilt top. Baste.

3 Quilt as desired.

4 Sew the 5 binding strips 2½″ × WOF together, end to end, with a diagonal seam. Bind and enjoy your finished table topper!

Buoyant Hearts

FINISHED BLOCK SIZE OF THE OUTER HEARTS: 8″ × 8″ ⚓ **FINISHED QUILT SIZE: 40½″ × 54″**

Buoyant Hearts takes advantage of the length of Jelly Roll strips by placing them in the background and superimposing rows of bobbing hearts on them. To distribute the fabrics and colors evenly, all **40** strips of a Jelly Roll are used in this design, creating more scraps than the other projects. I recommend using those scraps in a *Neighborly* (page 16) wall hanging.

Fabric Requirements

Instructions presume at least a 40″ width of fabric (WOF) after removing the selvages.

- 40 Jelly Roll strips for the background
- 1⅓ yards off-white fabric for the outer hearts
- ⅓ yard burgundy fabric for the inner hearts
- 2⅞ yards backing
- ⅝ yard binding
- 49″ × 62″ batting

Cutting

JELLY ROLL STRIPS

Divide the Jelly Roll strips into 6 groups, distributing the colors equally among them:
  1 with 12 strips
  1 with 8 strips
  2 with 6 strips
  2 with 4 strips

From each strip in the group with **12 strips**, cut:
  1 A rectangle 2½″ × 12½″
  1 A square 2″ × 2″
  1 B rectangle 2½″ × 4½″
  1 B square 2½″ × 2½″
  1 B square 2″ × 2″

From each strip in the group with **8 strips**, cut:
  1 C rectangle 2½″ × 10″
  1 C square 2″ × 2″
  1 B rectangle 2½″ × 4½″
  1 B square 2½″ × 2½″
  1 B square 2″ × 2″

From each strip in the 1st group with **4 strips**, cut:
  1 D rectangle 2½″ × 14½″
  1 D square 2½″ × 2½″
  1 E rectangle 2½″ × 6½″
  1 E square 2½″ × 2½″
  1 E square 2″ × 2″

From each strip in the 1st group with **6 strips**, cut:
  1 F rectangle 2½″ × 12″
  1 F square 2½″ × 2½″
  1 E rectangle 2½″ × 6½″
  1 E square 2½″ × 2½″
  1 E square 2″ × 2″

Pieced by
Michelle Cain

Quilted by
Ophelia Chang

Social media:
#BuoyantHeartsQuilt

FABRICS USED
Jelly Roll: Songbook by Fancy That
Design House for Moda
Heart fabrics: Moda Bella
Solids in Off-White and Burgundy

From each strip in the 2nd group with **6 strips**, cut:
  1 G rectangle 2½″ × 10″
  1 G square 2½″ × 2½″
  1 E rectangle 2½″ × 6½″
  1 E square 2½″ × 2½″
  1 E square 2″ × 2″
From each strip in the 2nd group with **4 strips**, cut:
  1 H rectangle 2½″ × 12½″
  1 H square 2½″ × 2½″
  1 E rectangle 2½″ × 6½″
  1 E square 2½″ × 2½″
  1 E square 2″ × 2″

Take all of the cut pieces and group by letter and then by shape. You should have:

- 12 of each size of A
- 20 of each size of B
- 8 of each size of C
- 4 of each size of D
- 20 of each size of E
- 6 of each size of F
- 6 of each size of G
- 4 of each size of H

OFF-WHITE FABRIC (OUTER HEARTS)
Cut 3 strips 4½″ × WOF.
  Subcut into 30 J rectangles 4½″ × 3″ (each strip can yield 13).
Cut 2 strips 2″ × WOF.
  Subcut into 30 K rectangles 2″ × 2½″ (each strip can yield 16).
Cut 6 strips 2½″ × WOF.
  Subcut into 90 L squares 2½″ × 2½″ (each strip can yield 16).
  From the scraps, subcut 4 M squares 1½″ × 1½″.
Cut 1 strip 1½″ × WOF.
  Subcut into 26 M squares 1½″ × 1½″ (for a total of 30 M squares).
Cut 1 strip 1″ × WOF.
  Subcut into 30 N squares 1″ × 1″.

BURGUNDY FABRIC (INNER HEARTS)
Cut 3 strips 2½″ × WOF.
  Subcut into 30 P rectangles 2½″ × 4″ (each strip can yield 10).

BINDING
Cut 6 strips 2½″ × WOF.

Construction

All seams are a scant ¼″ unless otherwise indicated. Press the seams open. Be sure to label all the unit pieces as they're sewn. For more specifics on the techniques used in this pattern, see Sewing Half-Square Triangles (page 13) and Snowballing Corners (page 14).

Snowball the Outer Hearts

A/J UNITS

1 Using 2 A squares 2″ × 2″, snowball the corners on a long side of a J rectangle. Trim and press.

2 Repeat to make a total of 6.

3 Sew 2 A/J units together. Press.

4 Repeat to make a total of 3.

A/J Units

steps 1–2

Sew 6.

steps 3–4

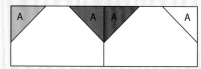

Sew 3.

B/E/J UNITS

For the steps and figures that follow, pay attention to the placement of the B and E fabrics.

1 Using 1 B square 2″ × 2″ and 1 E square 2″ × 2″, snowball the corners on a long side of a J rectangle, as indicated in the figure. Trim and press.

2 Repeat to make a total of 10.

3 Using 1 B square 2″ × 2″ and 1 E square 2″ × 2″, snowball the corners of a long side of a J rectangle, as indicated in the figure. Trim and press.

4 Repeat to make a total of 10.

5 Sew a B/E/J unit from Step 1 with a B/E/J unit from Step 3, as indicated in the figure. Press.

6 Repeat to make a total of 10.

C/J UNITS

1 Using 2 C squares 2″ × 2″, snowball the corners of a long side of a J rectangle. Trim and press.

2 Repeat to make a total of 4.

3 Sew 2 C/J units together. Press.

4 Repeat to make a total of 2.

Sew the Half-Square Triangles

1 Gather the pieces to make half-square triangles (HSTs) in the following combinations and quantities (each pair of 1 Jelly Roll square 2½″ × 2½″ and 1 L square produces 1 finished HST):

    20 B/L HSTs

    4 D/L HSTs

    20 E/L HSTs

    6 F/L HSTs

    6 G/L HSTs

    4 H/L HSTs

2 Sew, trim, and press each HST.

B/E/J Units

steps 1–2

Sew 10.

steps 3–4

Sew 10.

steps 5–6

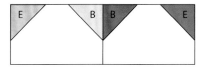

Sew 10.

C/J Units

steps 1–2

Sew 4.

steps 3–4

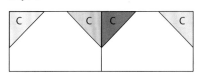

Sew 2.

Sew the Half-Square Triangles

step 2

Sew the Inner Heart Units

1 Using an L, an M, and an N square, snowball the corners of a P rectangle as indicated in the diagram. Trim and press. This is the left side of an inner heart.

2 Repeat to make a total of 15.

3 Using an L, an M, and an N square, snowball the corners of a P rectangle as indicated in the diagram. Trim and press. This is the right side of an inner heart.

4 Repeat to make a total of 15.

5 Sew a left side and a right side together to make a full heart. Press.

6 Repeat to make a total of 15.

Arrange the Columns

There are 2 different column designs. A design wall or adequate floor space will make laying out the pieces easier.

COLUMN 1

For the following steps, refer to the Column 1 Assembly Diagram (page 39).

1 Lay out 1 A/J heart top and 2 B/E/J heart tops. Fill in with the following pieces, making sure that the fabrics match those in the adjacent heart units:

4 A rectangles	4 E rectangles
4 B rectangles	4 E/L HSTs
4 B/L HSTs	

2 To the layout, add the following pieces:

2 F rectangles	2 G/L HSTs
2 F/L HSTs	6 K rectangles
2 G rectangles	

COLUMN 2

For the following steps, refer to the Column 2 Assembly Diagram (page 39).

1 Lay out 1 C/J heart top and 2 B/E/J heart tops. Fill in with the following pieces, making sure that the fabrics match those in the adjacent heart tops:

4 C rectangles	4 E rectangles
4 B rectangles	4 E/L HSTs
4 B/L HSTs	

2 To the layout, add the following pieces:

2 D rectangles	2 H/L HSTs
2 D/L HSTs	6 K rectangles
2 H rectangles	

Sew the Inner Heart Units

steps 1–2

 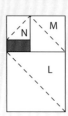 

Sew 15.

steps 3–4

 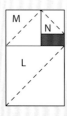 

Sew 15.

steps 5–6

Sew 15.

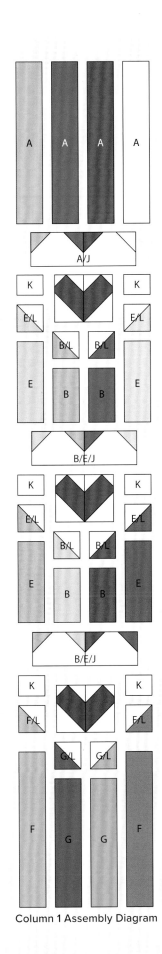

Column 1 Assembly Diagram

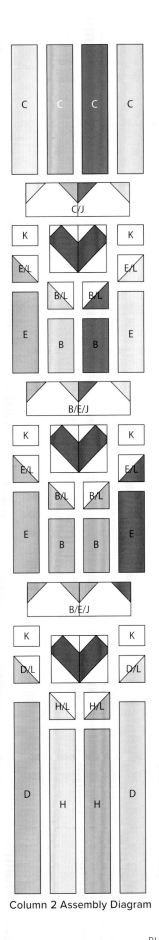

Column 2 Assembly Diagram

Sew the Columns

Refer to the Column Assembly Diagrams for the letter labels of the pieces. Although the lengths of the rectangles differ, each heart section is sewn in the same order.

1 Sew the K rectangles to the HSTs below them. Press.

2 Sew all the HSTs to the rectangles below them. Press.

3 Sew the inner units together. Press.

4 Sew the inner unit to the inner heart above it. Press.

5 Sew the pieces into rows. Press.

6 Sew the rows into a completed column, 54″ in length. Press.

7 Repeat Steps 1–6 to sew 3 of Column 1 and 2 of Column 2.

Assemble the Top

For the following steps, refer to the Quilt Assembly Diagram.

1 The completed quilt top follows this configuration: Column 1 + Column 2 + Column 1 + Column 2 + Column 1.

2 Start by placing pins in spots where a Column 1 outer heart seam intersects a Column 2 outer heart seam. Then insert pins every 1½″–2″. Sew and press.

3 Continue this process until the 5 columns are sewn together.

> ✳ *Tip* ✳
>
> To secure the seams along the perimeter of the quilt top, take a victory lap! That is, stay stitch ⅛″ away from the edge on all 4 sides.

Sew the Columns

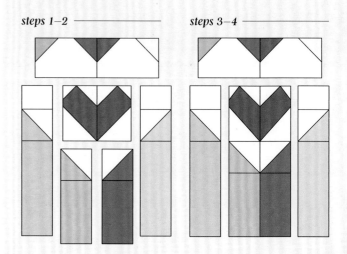

steps 1–2   steps 3–4

Assemble the Top

Column 1   Column 2   Column 1   Column 2   Column 1

Quilt Assembly Diagram

Finishing the Quilt

For more details on completing a quilt, see Finishing the Projects (page 108).

1 To make the backing, cut the 2⅞ yards backing fabric into 2 strips 49″ × WOF. Using a ½″ seam allowance, sew the 2 strips together along the long edges. Press the seam open. Trim to approximately 49″ × 62″.

2 Build the quilt sandwich: backing + batting + quilt top. Baste.

3 Quilt as desired.

4 Sew the 6 binding strips 2½″ × WOF together, end to end, with a diagonal seam. Bind and enjoy your finished quilt!

Pod Patrol

FINISHED BLOCK SIZE: 14″ × 6″ ✦ **FINISHED QUILT SIZE: 56½″ × 66½″**

This pod isn't a gathering of your average whales—these cuties swim the pixelated seas! Each member of *Pod Patrol* requires a single strip, leaving the balance of your Jelly Roll to make striped or scrappy waves.

Fabric Requirements

Instructions presume at least a 40″ width of fabric (WOF) after removing the selvages.

- 34 Jelly Roll strips
    10 for the whales
    24 for the waves (6 in each of 4 different colorways)*
- 1¼″ × 12½″ scrap of red fabric for the mouths
- ¾″ × 7½″ scrap of white fabric for the eyes
- ¼ yard blue fabric for the bellies
- 2¾ yards background fabric
- 3¾ yards backing
- 65″ × 75″ batting

- ⅝ yard binding
- 6″ × 6″ piece of thick template plastic
- 1 photocopy or printout of the 2 half-rectangle triangle templates (page 111)
- Glue stick
- Craft scissors

* See the sidebar, Alternative Wave Designs, for different options to create the waves.

ALTERNATIVE WAVE DESIGNS

If you're short on time, forgo the pixelated waves. Instead, buy ⅝ yard of 2 different fabrics. (If you want to match the repeat of a print design, you may need more than that.) Cut both into 3 strips 6½″ × WOF. Sew the 3 strips of 1 fabric together, end to end. From that long strip, cut 2 waves 6½″ × 56½″. Do the same for the 2nd fabric. Use these swaths of fabric in place of the pixelated waves in the pattern.

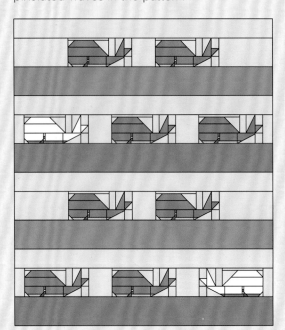

Or, if you like the pixelated look but your Jelly Roll doesn't contain enough strips in 4 different colorways, you can create scrappy waves. Cut 21 Jelly Roll strips into 42 strips 2½″ × 20″. Then sew 3 Jelly Roll strips 2½″ × 20″ together along the long edges. Press the seams in the same direction.

Repeat with the remaining 39 strips, for a total of 14 strip sets. Cut the sets into 112 wave units 2½″ × 6½″ (each set can yield 8). Sew 4 bands of 28 units each, rotating the units to nest the seams.

Pieced by
Michelle Cain

Quilted by
Ophelia Chang

Social media:
#PodPatrolQuilt

FABRICS USED
Jelly Roll: Water from
Ruby Star Society
Background fabric: Moda
Bella Solids in Smoke

Template Preparation

Pod Patrol *requires templates (page 111) to cut and sew half-rectangle triangles (HRTs). Unlike half-square triangles, HRTs have an orientation, and* Pod Patrol *requires both a left HRT and a right HRT template.*

Photocopy or print out the HRT templates and cut each along the outer dashed lines. Adhere them to the plastic with a glue stick. Cut out both templates.

Left HRT Right HRT

Cutting

JELLY ROLL STRIPS

Keep the pieces from 1 Jelly Roll strip together.

From each of 10 Jelly Roll strips for the whales, cut:
  1 rectangle 2½″ × 9½″
  1 rectangle 2½″ × 4½″
Trim the remnants down to 2¼″ × the remaining WOF, and cut from each:
  1 square 2¼″ × 2¼″
Trim the remnants down to 2″ × the remaining WOF, and cut from each:
  1 rectangle 2″ × 9½″
  1 strip 2″ × 14″

RED FABRIC (MOUTHS)
Cut 10 squares 1¼″ × 1¼″.

WHITE FABRIC (EYES)
Cut 10 squares ¾″ × ¾″.

BLUE FABRIC (BELLIES)
Cut 5 strips 1″ × WOF.
  Subcut into 10 strips 1″ × 14¼″ (each strip can yield 2).

✳ *Tip* ✳

The Whale blocks produce few scraps. Cut with caution, or better yet, sew a test block.

BACKGROUND FABRIC

Blocks

Cut 2 strips 4½″ × WOF.
  Subcut 1 strip into 16 A rectangles 4½″ × 2½″.
  Subcut 1 strip into 4 A rectangles 4½″ × 2½″ (for a total of 20 A rectangles and 10 B rectangles 4½″ × 1¾″.
Cut 1 strip 4″ × WOF.
  Subcut into 10 C squares 4″ × 4″.
Cut 2 strips 2¼″ × WOF.
  Subcut 1 strip into 10 D rectangles 2¼″ × 2¾″ and 5 E rectangles 2¼″ × 2½″.
  Subcut 1 strip into 5 E rectangles 2¼″ × 2½″ (for a total of 10 E rectangles) and 10 F squares 2¼″ × 2¼″.
Cut 1 strip 2″ × WOF.
  Subcut into 10 G squares 2″ × 2″ and 10 H squares 1½″ × 1½″.
Cut 3 strips 1″ × WOF.
  Subcut into 10 J rectangles 1″ × 9½″ (each strip can yield 4).

Spacers

Cut 3 strips 6½″ × WOF.
  Subcut 1 strip into 6 K rectangles 6½″ × 5½″.
  Subcut 2 strips into 4 L rectangles 6½″ × 14″ and 4 M rectangles 6½″ × 4½″ (each strip can yield 2 rectangles of each size).

Sashing

Cut 6 strips 5″ × WOF.

BINDING
Cut 7 strips 2½″ × WOF.

Construction

All seams are a scant ¼" unless otherwise indicated. Press the seams open unless directed to press to the side. For more specifics on the techniques used in this pattern, see Sewing Half-Square Triangles (page 13), Snowballing Corners (page 14), and Working with Strip Sets (page 14).

Make the Left-Facing Whales

All but 1 of the whales in the pattern face to the left.

SEW THE HEAD UNIT

1 Gather the pieces for a Whale block cut from 1 Jelly Roll strip.

2 Sew the 2½" × 9½" whale rectangle to the 2" × 9½" whale rectangle along a long side. Press.

3 Snowball the top left corner of the unit with a G square and the top right corner with a C square. Trim, reserving the larger triangular Jelly Roll scrap, and press.

4 Sew a J rectangle onto the top of the unit. Press.

SEW THE BELLY UNIT

1 From the triangular Jelly Roll scrap, cut 1 rectangle ¾" × 1¼" and 1 rectangle ¾" × 1".

2 Sew an eye square in between the pieces cut in Step 1. Press the seams away from the eye square.

3 Sew the unit to the end of the whale strip 2" × 14" as indicated in the figure and with the 1¼" rectangle on top. Press.

4 Sew a belly strip onto the bottom of the unit. Press.

5 As indicated in the figure, cut the unit into 3 segments: 1 rectangle 2½" × 4¾" and 2 rectangles 2½" × 4½".

6 Using an H square and a mouth square, snowball the bottom corners of 1 rectangle 2½" × 4½" as indicated in the figure.

7 Place the *left HRT template* on the other rectangle 2½" × 4½", with the fabric right side up, as indicated in the figure. Cut out the triangle, trimming the angles at the points. Do the same with an A rectangle.

Sew the Head Unit

step 2

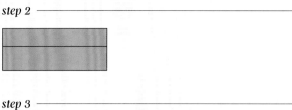

step 3

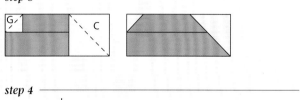

step 4

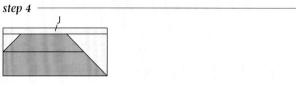

Sew the Belly Unit

step 1   *step 2*

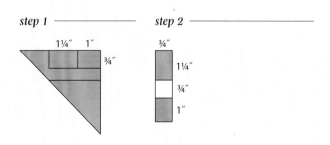

step 3

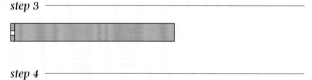

step 4

step 5

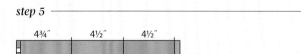

step 6

step 7

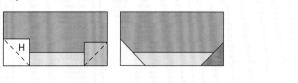

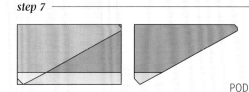

8 Match up the angled points of the 2 triangles from Step 7, as indicated in the figure. Sew and press. The HRT will measure 2½″ × 4½″ (unfinished).

SEW THE TAIL UNIT

1 Place the *right HRT template* on the whale rectangle 2½″ × 4½″, with the fabric right side up, as indicated in the figure. Cut out the triangle, trimming the angles at the points. Do the same with an A rectangle.

2 Match up the angled points of the 2 triangles from Step 1, as indicated in the figure. Sew and press. The HRT will measure 2½″ × 4½″ (unfinished).

3 Sew 1 half-square triangle using the whale square 2¼″ × 2¼″ and 1 F square. Trim and press.

4 Sew a D rectangle to the half-square triangle as indicated in the figure. Press.

COMPLETE THE WHALE

1 Lay out the pieces of a block as indicated in the figure.

2 Sew the pieces into 2 rows. Press.

3 Sew the 2 rows together. Press.

4 Repeat all the steps for Sew the Head Unit, Sew the Belly Unit, and Sew the Tail Unit to complete a total of 9 left-facing whales.

step 8

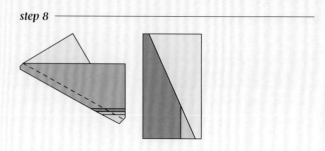

Sew the Tail Unit

step 1

step 2

step 3   *step 4*

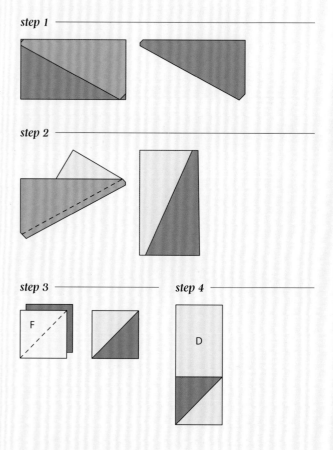

Complete the Whale

step 1

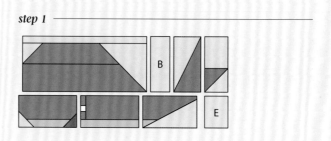

Make the Right-Facing Whale

The single right-facing whale has all the same pieces as its left-facing counterpart; they're just oriented in the opposite direction. For the right-facing whale, repeat the steps under Sew the Head Unit, Sew the Belly Unit, and Sew the Tail Unit with the following modifications.

1 Assemble the head with pieces oriented as indicated in the figure.

2 Sew the belly, placing the eye unit on the opposite end of the unit as the left-facing whales, and cut the segments as indicated.

3 Using an H square and a mouth square, snowball the bottom corners of 1 rectangle 2½″ × 4½″ as indicated in the figure.

4 Cut 1 rectangle 2½″ × 4½″ from Step 2 using the *right HRT template*. Cut an A rectangle with the same template. Sew the 2 triangles together.

5 Cut the whale rectangle 2½″ × 4½″ using the *left HRT template*. Cut an A rectangle using the same template. Sew the 2 triangles together.

6 Sew the pieces into rows, and then sew the rows together.

Make the Waves

The instructions that follow create striped waves. See the accompanying sidebar, Alternative Wave Designs (page 42), for other options.

SEW THE STRIP SETS

1 Using the 24 Jelly Roll strips for the waves, sew 2 strip sets in each of the combinations shown in the figure, and press the seams to 1 side as indicated.

2 Cut each of the strip sets into 16 wave units 2½″ × 6½″, for a total of 128 units.

ASSEMBLE THE WAVES

1 Lay out 28 wave units 2½″ × 6½″ as indicated in the figure, positioning them so that the seams of adjacent units nest.

2 Repeat with the remaining wave units to create 4 bands of 28 units. (There will be 16 extra units.)

Make the Right-Facing Whale

step 1

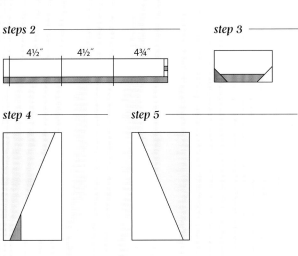

steps 2 — 4½″ 4½″ 4¾″

step 3

step 4 *step 5*

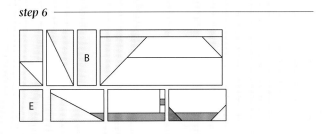

step 6

B

E

Sew the Strip Sets

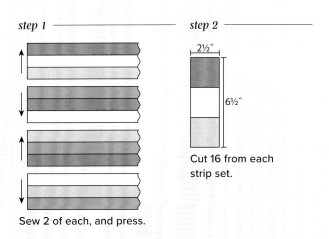

step 1

step 2 — 2½″ 6½″

Cut 16 from each strip set.

Sew 2 of each, and press.

Assemble the Waves

step 1

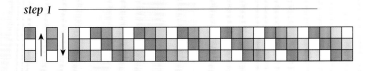

Assemble the Top

Refer to the Row Assembly Diagram and Quilt Assembly Diagram for the remaining construction steps.

SEW THE WHALES TOGETHER

1 Sew a K rectangle in between 2 left-facing Whale blocks. Press.

2 Repeat for a total of 4 rows of 2 left-facing Whale blocks.

3 Sew an additional K rectangle and a Whale block on the end of 2 of those rows. Press.

4 To the 2 rows of 2 Whale blocks, sew an L rectangle on each end. Press.

5 To the 2 rows of 3 Whale blocks, sew an M rectangle on each end. Press.

SEW THE SASHING

1 Measure the length of each band of waves, and calculate the average length. (It should be about 56½˝.)

2 Sew the 6 sashing strips 5˝ × WOF together, end to end.

3 From that long strip, cut 4 lengths, using the measurement from Step 1.

SEW THE ROWS TOGETHER

The rows of whales are purposefully longer than 56½˝. They need to be trimmed before assembling the quilt top.

1 Trim each row of whales to the measurement calculated for Sew the Sashing. Take the same amount off each end of a row to center the whales horizontally on the quilt.

2 Lay out the rows of whales, bands of waves, and sashing as indicated in the Quilt Assembly Diagram.

3 Pin liberally, and sew the rows together. Press.

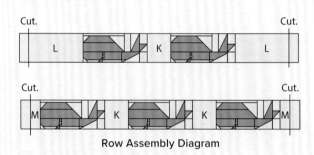

Row Assembly Diagram

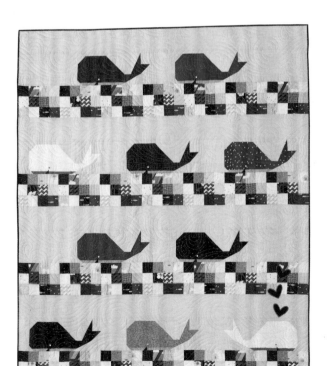

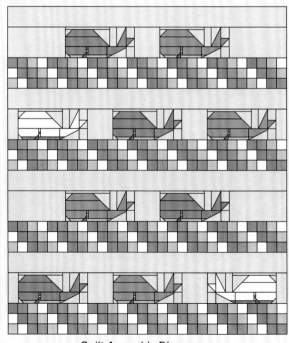

Quilt Assembly Diagram

Finishing the Quilt

For more details on completing a quilt, see Finishing the Projects (page 108).

1 To make the backing, cut the 3¾ yards backing fabric into 2 strips 65″ × WOF. Using a ½″ seam allowance, sew the 2 strips together along the long edges. Press the seam open. Trim to approximately 65″ × 75″.

2 Build the quilt sandwich: backing + batting + quilt top. Baste.

3 Quilt as desired.

4 Sew the 7 binding strips 2½″ × WOF together, end to end, with a diagonal seam. Bind and enjoy your finished quilt!

APPLIQUÉING THE HEART SPRAY

After quilting *Pod Patrol*, I added some appliquéd hearts to my right-facing whale. There are many different ways to appliqué on a quilt. I chose a raw-edge technique with an imperfect-on-purpose straight stitch.

1 Purchase an iron-on adhesive appropriate for appliqué. (I had HeatnBond Lite on hand, but there are many comparable products on the market.)

2 Place the adhesive, paper side up, on the heart template (page 111), and trace it as many times as desired.

3 Using craft scissors, rough-cut around each shape, about ¼ inch outside of the lines.

4 Following the directions on the product packaging, use an iron to adhere the hearts (paper side up) to the wrong side of the fabric you're using to appliqué.

5 Once the hearts are cool, cut them out along the traced lines.

6 Peel off the paper, and place the hearts adhesive side down on the quilt top. Iron to bond them to the quilt top.

7 Machine-stitch around each shape a few times. Don't strive for perfection, sewing each new round of stitches directly on the last. A messy-on-purpose approach works well here.

Meow Mates

FINISHED BLOCK SIZE: 10″ × 10″ ⚜ **FINISHED QUILT SIZE: 52½″ × 64½″**

I designed *Meow Mates* to bust through leftover low-volume strips, and the version pictured here contains selections from many of the other projects in this book. I focused on prints with small florals, ginghams, and polka dots—for both the cat faces and the accents—to create the finished quilt's vintage vibe. Then, for some much-needed variety amid all the low-volume fabrics, I incorporated darker solids from my scrap bin.

Fabric Requirements

Instructions presume at least a 40″ width of fabric (WOF) after removing the selvages. The fabric requirements call for single fabrics for each of the cats' features, and the colors listed below correspond to the colors in the accompanying illustrations. The sample quilt, however, was sewn with lots of scraps. See the sidebar Make It Scrappy for more information.

- 20 Jelly Roll strips for the cat faces
- ½ yard light pink fabric for the ears
- ⅛ yard or scrap of black fabric for the eyes
- ⅛ yard or scrap of dark pink fabric for the noses
- ⅜ yard gray fabric for the muzzles
- 2⅛ yards background fabric
- 3½ yards backing
- 61″ × 73″ batting
- ⅝ yard binding

MAKE IT SCRAPPY

Mixing up the fabrics in this design is easy. Each cat face requires a full Jelly Roll strip, so the pattern can accommodate unused strips you have on hand. To sew the ears, eyes, noses, and muzzles with scraps, as I did for the sample, you will need pieces that are these sizes:

A pair of ears: 4 squares 2½″ × 2½″

A pair of eyes: 1 rectangle 2½″ × 1¼″

A nose: 2 squares 1¼″ × 1¼″

A muzzle: 2 rectangles 2½″ × 3″

Cutting

JELLY ROLL STRIPS
From each of 20 Jelly Roll strips, cut:
   2 A rectangles 2½″ × 10½″
   2 B rectangles 2½″ × 2¼″
   1 C rectangle 2½″ × 1¾″
   1 D rectangle 2½″ × 5½″
   2 E rectangles 2½″ × 3″

LIGHT PINK FABRIC (EARS)
Cut 5 strips 2½″ × WOF.
   Subcut into 80 squares 2½″ × 2½″ (each strip can yield 16).

BLACK FABRIC (EYES)
Cut 1 strip 2½″ × WOF.
   Subcut into 20 rectangles 2½″ × 1¼″.

DARK PINK FABRIC (NOSES)
Cut 2 strips 1¼″ × WOF.
   Subcut into 40 squares 1¼″ × 1¼″ (each strip can yield 32).

GRAY FABRIC (MUZZLES)
Cut 4 strips 2½″ × WOF.
   Subcut into 40 rectangles 2½″ × 3″ (each strip can yield 13).

BACKGROUND FABRIC

Blocks
Cut 10 strips 2½″ × WOF.*
   Subcut 7 strips into 20 rectangles 2½″ × 10½″ (each strip can yield 3).
   Subcut 3 strips into 40 squares 2½″ × 2½″ (each strip can yield 16).

   * Note: If the usable fabric after removing selvages is at least 42″, cut just 8 strips. Use 5 to cut the rectangles (each strip can yield 4) and 3 to cut the squares (each strip can yield 16).

Sashing
Cut 9 strips 2½″ × WOF.

Borders
Cut 6 strips 3½″ × WOF.

BINDING
Cut 7 strips 2½″ × WOF.

Pieced by
Michelle Cain

Quilted by
Ophelia Chang

Social media:
#MeowMatesQuilt

FABRICS USED
Jelly Roll: Prints and solids from
various fabric collections
Background fabric: Moda Bella
Solids in Hometown Sky

Construction

All seams are a scant ¼″ unless otherwise indicated. Press the seams open except for the few spots that are marked with arrows and will facilitate nesting. For more specifics on snowballing, see Snowballing Corners (page 14).

Sew the Ear Units

1 Snowball a background rectangle with 2 ear squares as indicated in the figure. Trim and press.

2 Repeat to make a total of 20 ear top units.

3 Divide the 40 A rectangles into 2 identical piles (that is, each print should appear the same number of times in each pile). Set 1 pile aside. Snowball 1 A rectangle from the pile at hand with 2 ear squares as indicated in the figure. Take care to trim exactly ¼″ from the sewn seams, and reserve the resulting Jelly Roll triangles for later. Press the seams.

4 Repeat with the remaining A rectangles in the pile at hand to make a total of 20 ear bottom units.

Sew the Chin Units

1 Gather the 2nd pile of A rectangles. Snowball an A rectangle with 2 background squares as indicated in the figure. Take care to trim exactly ¼″ from the sewn seams, and reserve the resulting Jelly Roll triangles for later. Press the seams.

2 Repeat to make a total of 20 chin units.

Sew the Eye Units

1 Sew an eye rectangle to a C rectangle. Press.

2 Cut the resulting piece into 2 eye/C units 1¼″ × 2½″ as indicated in the figure.

3 Repeat Step 1 to sew a total of 20 pieces. Then, following Step 2, cut those pieces into a total of 40 eye/C units.

Sew the Ear Units

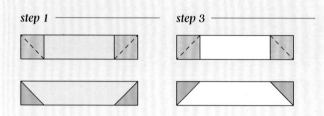

step 1   step 3

Sew the Chin Units

step 1

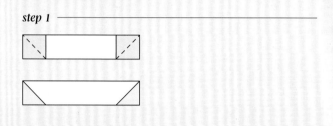

Sew the Eye Units

step 1   step 2

1¼″ 1¼″

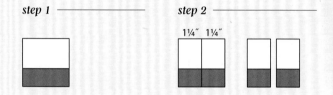

Sew the Muzzle Units

1 Gather the Jelly Roll triangles set aside earlier. From each triangle, cut 1 square 1″ × 1″, for a total of 80 squares (4 of each of the 20 prints used for the cat faces).

2 Select 4 squares 1″ × 1″ in the same Jelly Roll print.

3 Using 2 of those squares 1″ × 1″ and 1 nose square, snowball a muzzle rectangle as indicated in the figure. Trim and press. This is the left half of the muzzle.

4 Using the remaining 2 squares in that print and 1 nose square, snowball a muzzle rectangle as indicated in the figure. Trim and press. This is the right half of the muzzle.

5 Sew the left and right halves together to create a finished muzzle. Press.

6 Repeat Steps 2–5 to sew a total of 20 muzzle units.

Complete the Blocks

1 Lay out a block as indicated in the figure.

2 Sew the eye row and the muzzle row. Press the seams to the side as indicated in the figure.

3 Sew the rows together. Press.

4 Repeat Steps 1–3 to make a total of 20 blocks.

Assemble the Top

For the remaining steps, refer to the Quilt Assembly Diagram, page 54.

SEW THE SASHING

1 Sew the 9 sashing strips 2½″ × WOF together, end to end. Press the seams.

2 From the resulting long strip, cut 15 vertical sashing rectangles 2½″ × 10½″. Set the rest aside.

3 Sew 3 vertical sashing rectangles 2½ × 10½″ in between 4 blocks to create a row. Press.

4 Repeat Step 3 to sew a total of 5 rows.

5 Measure each row, and calculate the average length. (It should be about 46½″.)

6 Cut 4 horizontal sashing strips that length from the strip set aside in Step 2.

7 Sew the horizontal sashing strips in between the rows. Press.

Sew the Muzzle Units

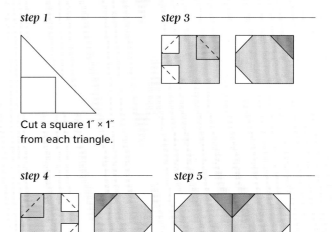

step 1

Cut a square 1″ × 1″ from each triangle.

step 3

step 4

step 5

Complete the Blocks

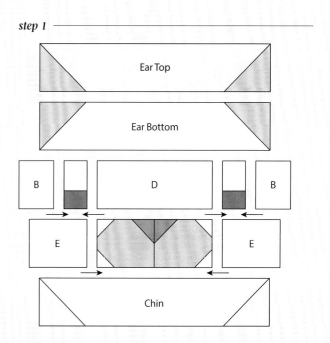

step 1

Ear Top

Ear Bottom

B   D   B

E   E

Chin

ADD THE BORDERS

1 Sew the 6 background strips 3½″ × WOF together, end to end. Press the seams.

2 Measure the quilt top at 3 points (each side and the middle) to find the average length. (It should be about 58½″.)

3 Cut 2 strips that length from the long strip. Sew those strips on the sides of the quilt top. Press.

4 Measure the quilt top at 3 points (the top, bottom, and middle) to find the average width. (It should be about 52½″.)

5 Cut 2 strips that width from the long strip. Sew those strips on the top and bottom of the quilt. Press.

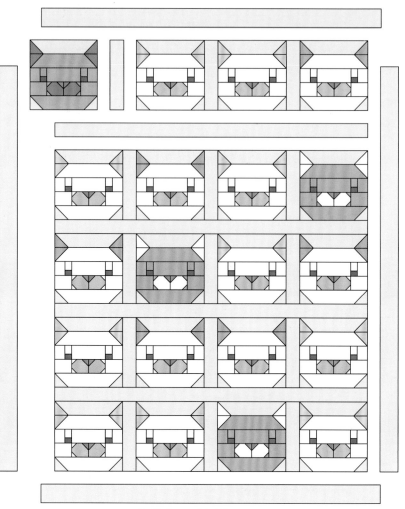

Quilt Assembly Diagram

Finishing the Quilt

For more details on completing a quilt, see Finishing the Projects (page 108).

1 To make the backing, cut the 3½ yards backing fabric into 2 strips 61″ × WOF. Using a ½″ seam allowance, sew the 2 strips together along the long edges. Press the seam open. Trim to approximately 61″ × 73″.

2 Build the quilt sandwich: backing + batting + quilt top. Baste.

3 Quilt as desired.

4 Sew the 7 binding strips 2½″ × WOF together, end to end, with a diagonal seam. Bind and enjoy your finished quilt!

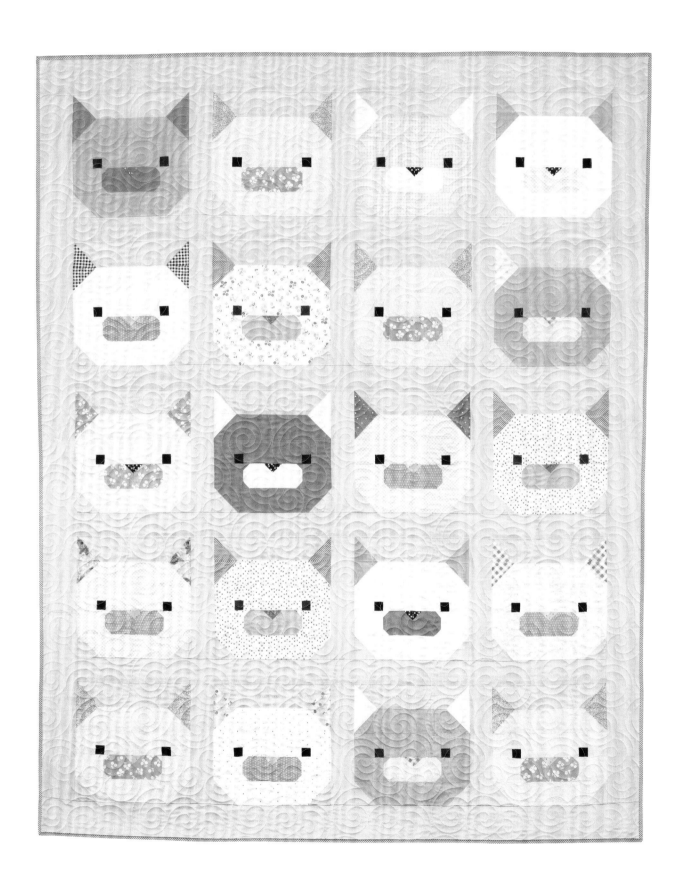

Step Dance

FINISHED BLOCK SIZE: 10″ × 10″ ❖ **FINISHED QUILT SIZE: 50½″ × 62½″**

Can Jelly Roll strips create an Irish chain quilt? Yes—and the outcome is decidedly modern!

A single Jelly Roll will probably not provide the necessary number of strips in four colorways, so get ready to raid your stash. For this version, I used two Jelly Rolls from Sweetwater for the foundation of my fabric pull and supplemented them with some stashed Basic Grey prints to flesh out the yellow colorway. The leftover low-volume Sweetwater strips became the basis for *Meow Mates* (page 50).

Fabric Requirements

Instructions presume at least a 40″ width of fabric (WOF) after removing the selvages.

- 36 Jelly Roll strips for the foreground (9 in each of 4 different colorways)
- 1¼ yards cream fabric for the background
- 3½ yards backing
- 59″ × 71″ batting
- ⅝ yard binding

Cutting

JELLY ROLL STRIPS (FOREGROUND FABRIC)
From each of the 4 colorways:
Cut **4 strips** into:
    2 rectangles 2½″ × 10½″
    2 rectangles 2½″ × 6½″
    2 squares 2½″ × 2½″
Cut **2 strips** into:
    1 rectangle 2½″ × 10½″
    3 rectangles 2½″ × 6½″
    2 squares 2½″ × 2½″
Cut **3 strips** into:
    1 rectangle 2½″ × 10½″
    2 rectangles 2½″ × 6½″
    3 squares 2½″ × 2½″
These cutting instructions produce in each colorway:
    13 rectangles 2½″ × 10½″
    20 rectangles 2½″ × 6½″
    21 squares 2½″ × 2½″

CREAM FABRIC (BACKGROUND FABRIC)
Cut 14 strips 2½″ × WOF.
    Subcut into 210 squares 2½″ × 2½″ (each strip can yield 16).

BINDING
Cut 7 strips 2½″ × WOF.

Pieced by
Michelle Cain

Quilted by
Ophelia Chang

Social media:
#StepDanceQuilt

FABRICS USED
Jelly Roll: Vintage by Sweetwater
for Moda
Background fabric: Moda Bella
Solids in Porcelain

Construction

All seams are a scant ¼″ unless otherwise indicated. Press seams to 1 side as illustrated by the arrows unless instructions indicate to press open.

Sew the Nine-Patch Blocks

1 To make a nine-patch block, lay out 4 foreground squares and 5 background squares as indicated in the figure. Sew them into rows. Press the seams to the foreground fabrics. Then sew the rows together, and press open.

2 See the figure for the 4 color combinations of nine-patch blocks to sew. Make 5 of each combination, for a total of 20. (There will be 4 extra foreground squares.)

Sew the Nine-Patch Blocks

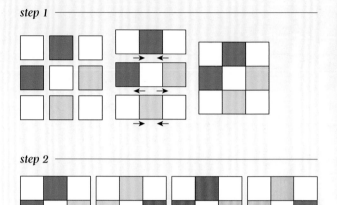

step 1

step 2

Make 5 of each.

USING DIRECTIONAL FABRICS

A print or two with a strong linear geometry works especially well with this pattern. A vertical stripe, for example, will accentuate the piecing and make the design resemble ascending stairs. (The sample quilt has some directional fabrics, but they're not quite bold enough to create the same effect.)

If you're using such a fabric, pay attention to its placement in the nine-patches. The foreground squares on the left and right sides should be rotated counterclockwise 90 degrees, as indicated by the smiley faces in the illustration.

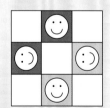

A mockup of *Step Dance* with some yellow and light blue striped fabric appears on the far right.

Complete the Blocks

1 Sew a rectangle 2½″ × 6½″ to both sides of each nine-patch block. (Be sure to match the color of the rectangles to the adjacent foreground squares.) Press the seams to the rectangles.

2 Sew a background square to both short sides of the remaining rectangles 2½″ × 6½″. Press the seams to the rectangles. There will be a total of 40 units.

3 Sew those 40 units on the top and bottom of the units from Step 1. (Be sure to match the color of the rectangles to the adjacent foreground squares). Press the seams to the newly added rectangles. There will be a total of 20 completed blocks.

Add the Vertical Sashing

1 Lay out the completed blocks as indicated in the figure.

2 Sew rectangles 2½″ × 10½″ in between the blocks as sashing to complete the 5 rows. (Be sure to match the color of those rectangles to the adjacent rectangles 2½″ × 6½″.) Press the seams to the sashing.

Sew the Horizontal Sashing

1 Using 16 rectangles 2½″ × 10½″ (4 of each colorway) and 12 background squares, sew the horizontal sashing as indicated. Press the seams to the foreground fabrics.

Complete the Blocks

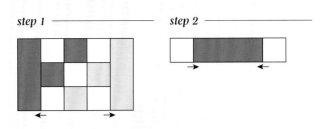

step 1   *step 2*

step 3

Add the Vertical Sashing

step 1

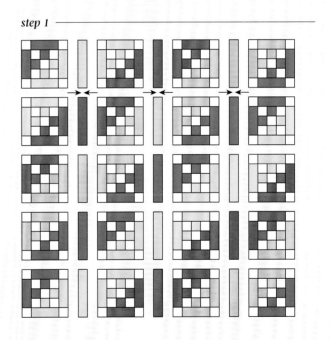

Sew the Horizontal Sashing

step 1

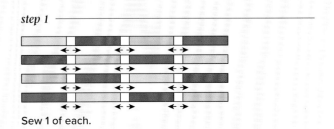

Sew 1 of each.

2 Sew the horizontal sashing in between the 5 rows. Press the seams to the sashing.

Sew the Borders

1 Using 4 rectangles 2½″ × 10½″ and 5 background squares for each, sew 2 different short borders, as indicated in the figure. Using 5 rectangles 2½″ × 10½″ and 4 background squares for each, sew 2 long borders with the same color configuration, as indicated in the figure. (There will be 3 extra rectangles 2½″ × 10½″.) Press the seams to the foreground fabrics.

2 Sew the 2 long borders on the sides of the quilt top. Press the seams to the outer edges.

3 Sew the 2 short borders on the top and bottom of the quilt top. Press the seams to the outer edges.

Finishing the Quilt

For more details on completing a quilt, see Finishing the Projects (page 108).

1 To make the backing, cut the 3½ yards of backing fabric into 2 strips 59″ × WOF. Using a ½″ seam allowance, sew the 2 strips together along the long edges. Press the seam open. Trim to approximately 59″ × 71″.

2 Build the quilt sandwich: backing + batting + quilt top. Baste.

3 Quilt as desired.

4 Sew the 7 binding strips 2½″ × WOF together, end to end, with a diagonal seam. Bind and enjoy your finished quilt!

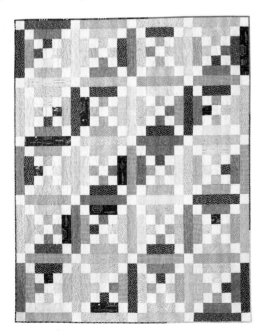

Sew the Horizontal Sashing

step 2

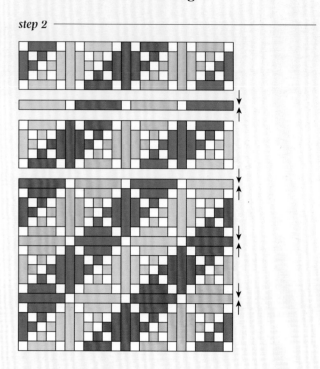

Sew the Borders

step 1

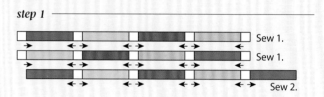

Sew 1.
Sew 1.
Sew 2.

steps 2–3

LARGE THROWS

Myriad

FINISHED BLOCK SIZE: 8″ high ⊕ FINISHED QUILT SIZE: 64½″ × 83¾″

Myriad's strip sets make this generously sized throw quilt come together quickly and easily.

This pattern requires a full 40-piece Jelly Roll. Because the one I used contained some low-volume prints that wouldn't work well with my white stars, I supplemented it with some strips cut from yardage of the same collection. Although my quilt is quite colorful, the illustrations use just two colors to help distinguish the two different block configurations.

Fabric Requirements

Instructions presume at least a 40″ width of fabric (WOF) after removing the selvages.

- 40 Jelly Roll strips for the hexagons
- 3¼ yards white fabric for the stars
- 5¼ yards backing
- 73″ × 92″ batting
- ¾ yard binding
- 12″ × 18″ piece of thick template plastic
- 2 photocopies or printouts of the small equilateral triangle and trapezoid templates (pages 110–111)
- 1 photocopy or printout of the right triangle template (page 110)
- Tape
- Glue stick
- Craft scissors

✳ *Tip* ✳

Starch can make this pattern's long strips and bias edges easier to sew accurately and without distortion. If you choose to starch and press the yardage and strips, do so before cutting.

Template Preparation

Myriad *requires templates (pages 110–111).*

Take 2 photocopies or printouts of the small equilateral triangle and trapezoid templates and 1 photocopy or printout of the right triangle template. Cut each along the outer dashed lines. Tape 1 small equilateral triangle template and 1 trapezoid template together, overlapping the seam allowances and lining up the solid sewing lines, to create a large equilateral triangle template. (The template will be 8″ high, excluding seam allowances.)

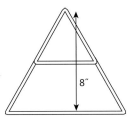

Make a large equilateral triangle template.

Adhere a small equilateral triangle, a large equilateral triangle, a trapezoid, and a right triangle template to the plastic with a glue stick. Cut out all 4 templates.

Glue all 4 templates onto the plastic and cut them out.

Pieced by
Michelle Cain

Quilted by
Ophelia Chang

Social media:
#MyriadQuilt

FABRICS USED
Jelly Roll: Confection Batiks by
Kate Spain for Moda
Star fabric: Moda Bella Solids in
White

Cutting

STAR FABRIC

The right triangle template will be used face up as well as face down to cut triangles of 2 different orientations.

Cut 8 strips 8½″ × WOF.

Subcut into 40 large equilateral triangles, 8 right triangles oriented one way, and 8 right triangles oriented the other way. Each strip can yield 5 large equilateral triangles and 2 right triangles (1 of each orientation) when configured like this:

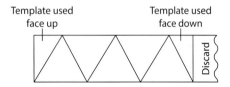

Cut 8 strips 4½″ × WOF.

Subcut into 96 small equilateral triangles. Each strip can yield 13 small equilateral triangles when configured like this:

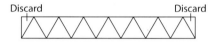

⁜ *Tip* ⁜

To make the cutting process go faster, stack multiple strips, and then, using a fresh rotary blade, cut the triangles.

BINDING

Cut 9 strips 2½″ × WOF.

Construction

All seams are a scant ¼″ unless otherwise indicated. Press the seams open. For more specifics on strip sets, see Working with Strip Sets (page 14).

⁜ *Tip* ⁜

To prevent bowing, shorten the stitch length to about 1.7mm (or 14–15 stitches per inch) before sewing the long strip sets.

Sew the Strip Sets

1 Sew 2 Jelly Roll strips together along the long edges. Press.

2 Repeat with the remaining 38 Jelly Roll strips, for a total of 20 strip sets.

Cut the Trapezoids

1 Using the trapezoid template, cut 1 strip set into 5 trapezoids as indicated in the figure.

2 Repeat with the remaining 19 strip sets, for a total of 100 trapezoids.

Add the Small Equilateral Triangles

1 Sew a small equilateral triangle to the top of a trapezoid. Press.

2 Repeat to create a total of 96 pieced triangles. (There will be 4 trapezoids left over.)

Cut the Trapezoids

step 1

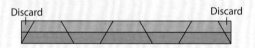

Add the Small Equilateral Triangles

step 1

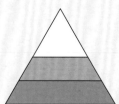

❈ *Tip* ❈

Take care not to distort the triangles' bias edges as you sew.

Sew the Pieced Triangles into Pairs

1 Sew 2 pieced triangles together as oriented in the figure. Press.

2 Repeat to create a total of 24 pairs.

3 Sew 2 pieced triangles together in the opposite orientation. Press.

4 Repeat to create a total of 24 pairs.

Sew the Pieced Triangles into Pairs

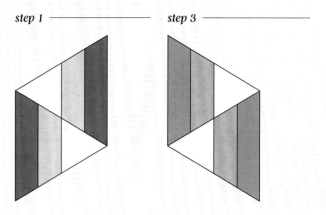

step 1 —————— *step 3* ——————

ACHIEVE PERFECT POINTS WITHOUT PINS

To get the seams to match up while sewing the pieced triangles into pairs, I recommend this trick:

1 Lay one pieced triangle on top of another, right sides together.

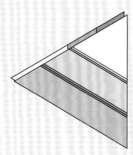

2 Carefully transfer them to your sewing machine, and sew five or six stitches just over the seams in question.

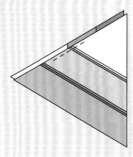

3 Take the pieces off the machine, open them up, and see whether you're pleased with their alignment. If you aren't, remove those few stitches, and try again. If you are, sew the entire seam, going directly over those initial starter stitches.

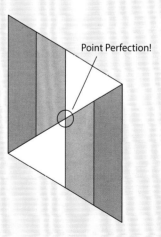

Point Perfection!

Assemble the Top

1 Following the Quilt Assembly Diagram, lay out the 48 pairs of pieced triangles with the right triangles and large equilateral triangles. (There are 2 different column configurations, labeled 1 and 2 in the diagram.)

2 Sew the blocks into 8 columns. Press.

3 Sew the columns together. Press.

Finishing the Quilt

For more details on completing a quilt, see Finishing the Projects (page 108).

1 To make the backing, cut the 5¼ yards backing fabric into 2 strips 92″ × WOF. Using a ½″ seam allowance, sew the 2 strips together along the long edges. Press the seam open. Trim to approximately 73″ × 92″.

2 Build the quilt sandwich: backing + batting + quilt top. Baste.

3 Quilt as desired.

4 Sew the 9 binding strips 2½″ × WOF together, end to end, with a diagonal seam. Bind and enjoy your finished quilt!

Quilt Assembly Diagram

Five-Star Experience

FINISHED BLOCK SIZE: 16″ × 16″ ✤ **FINISHED QUILT SIZE: 73½″ × 73½″**

Five-Star Experience, with its large, over-the-top blocks, is a fast and satisfying sew. The version pictured here gives off a scrappy vibe. Imagine the same design in a Christmas-themed fabric collection: Red prints with yellow accent squares would transform these stars into beautiful, oversize poinsettias.

Fabric Requirements

Instructions presume at least a 40″ width of fabric (WOF) after removing the selvages.

- 39 Jelly Roll strips
    32 for the star points
    4 for the accent squares
    3 for the backing*
- 4⅔ yards background fabric
- 4¾ yards backing
- 82″ × 82″ batting
- ¾ yard binding

> ** The 3 Jelly Roll strips minimize the amount of backing yardage required. If there are 41½″ of usable backing fabric after removing the selvages, these 3 Jelly Roll strips are not necessary. (See Finishing the Quilt, page 72.)*

Cutting

STAR POINTS

From each of the 32 Jelly Roll strips, cut:
    1 rectangle 2½″ × 14½″
    1 rectangle 2½″ × 12½″
    1 rectangle 2½″ × 10½″

ACCENT SQUARES

Cut 4 Jelly Roll strips into 51 squares 2½″ × 2½″ (each strip can yield 16).

BACKGROUND FABRIC

Blocks

Cut 6 strips 10½″ × WOF.*
    Subcut into 16 squares 10½″ × 10½″ (each strip can yield 3).

> ** Note: If the usable fabric after removing selvages is at least 42″, cut just 4 strips (each strip can yield 4).*

Cut 6 strips 6½″ × WOF.
    Subcut into 32 squares 6½″ × 6½″ (each strip can yield 6).

Sashing

Cut 11 strips 2½″ × WOF.

Borders

Cut 8 strips 2″ × WOF.

BINDING

Cut 9 strips 2½″ × WOF.

Pieced by Michelle Cain

Quilted by Ophelia Chang

Social media: #FiveStarExperienceQuilt

FABRICS USED
Jelly Roll: Meadow Star by Alexia Marcelle Abegg for Ruby Star Society
Accent fabric: Moda Bella Solids in Black
Background fabric: Speckled in Sweet Cream by Rashida Coleman Hale for Ruby Star Society

Construction

All seams are a scant ¼″ unless otherwise indicated. Press the seams open. For more specifics on snowballing, see Snowballing Corners (page 14).

Add the Accent Squares

1 Sew an accent square onto 16 rectangles 2½″ × 10½″, 16 rectangles 2½″ × 12½″, and 16 rectangles 2½″ × 14½″. Press.

Sew the Half Log Cabin Blocks

1 Sew a rectangle 2½″ × 10½″ onto a background square 10½″ × 10½″. Press.

2 Sew a rectangle 2½″ × 10½″ with an accent square to an adjacent side, positioning the accent square at the intersection of the 2 rectangles. Press.

3 Continue to add pieces on these 2 sides of the background square, alternating between plain rectangles and rectangles with an accent square.

4 Repeat Steps 1–3 with the remaining background squares 10½″ × 10½″, plain rectangles, and rectangles with an accent square. There will be a total of 16 Half Log Cabin blocks, each measuring 16½″ × 16½″ (unfinished).

Snowball the Points

1 Using 2 background squares 6½″ × 6½″, snowball the 2 pieced corners of a Half Log Cabin block. Trim and press.

2 Repeat with the remaining 15 Half Log Cabin blocks.

Add the Accent Squares

step 1

Sew 16 of each.

Sew the Half Log Cabin Blocks

step 1   *step 2*

step 3

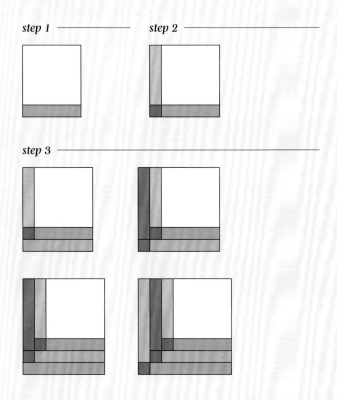

Snowball the Points

step 1

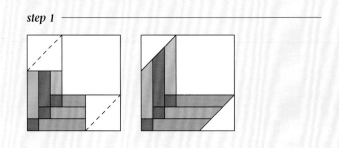

Complete the Full Stars

1 Sew the 11 background strips 2½″ × WOF together, end to end. Press the seams open.

2 From the resulting long strip, cut 14 strips 2½″ × 16½″. Set the rest aside.

3 Lay out 4 Half Log Cabin blocks as illustrated in the figure. Using 1 accent square 2½″ × 2½″ and 4 background strips 2½″ × 16½″, sew the pieces into rows. Press.

4 Sew the rows together. Press.

5 Repeat Steps 3–4 to make a total of 3 full stars. (The remaining 2 background strips 2½″ × 16½″ will be used in the next step.)

Complete the Partial Stars

1 Lay out 2 Half Log Cabin blocks as illustrated in the figure. Create a partial star by sewing a background strip 2½″ × 16½″ in between them. Press.

2 Repeat to make a total of 2 partial stars.

Assemble the Top

1 Using the remaining long 2½″ strip set aside earlier, cut 3 horizontal sashing strips 2½″ × 34½″.

2 Lay out the 3 full stars and 2 partial stars as indicated in the figure. Sew the 3 horizontal sashing strips in between the blocks to create 2 columns.

3 Measure the 2 columns and calculate the average length. (It should be about 70½″.) Cut 1 vertical sashing strip that length from the remaining 2½″ strip, and sew it in between the columns. Press.

4 Sew the 8 background strips 2″ × WOF together, end to end. Press the seams open.

5 Using the calculation from Step 3, cut 2 borders that length from the long strip from Step 4. Sew them on either side of the quilt top, as illustrated in the Quilt Assembly Diagram (page 72). Press.

Complete the Full Stars

step 3

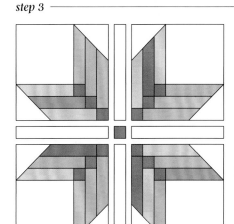

Complete the Partial Stars

step 1

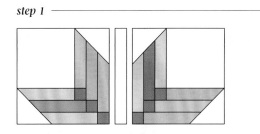

Assemble the Top

steps 2–3

6 Measure the quilt top at 3 points (the top, bottom, and middle) to find the average width. (It should be about 73½″.) Cut 2 borders that width from the remaining 2″ strip. Sew them on the top and bottom of the quilt, as illustrated in the Quilt Assembly Diagram. Press.

Finishing the Quilt

For more details on completing a quilt, see Finishing the Projects (page 108).

1 To make the backing, cut the 4¾ yards backing fabric into 2 strips 82″ × WOF.

If there are 41½″ of usable fabric after removing the selvages, sew the 2 strips together along the long edges using a ½″ seam allowance. Press the seam open. Trim to approximately 82″ × 82″.

If the fabric is narrower, sew the 3 Jelly Roll strips together, end to end, and press the seams. Using a ¼″ seam allowance, sew the 2 strips of yardage together along the long edges with the Jelly Roll strips in between. Press the seams open. Trim to approximately 82″ × 82″.

2 Build the quilt sandwich: backing + batting + quilt top. Baste.

3 Quilt as desired.

4 Sew the 9 binding strips 2½″ × WOF together, end to end, with a diagonal seam. Bind and enjoy your finished quilt!

Quilt Assembly Diagram

Finishing the Quilt

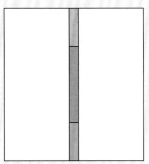

Backing pieced with Jelly Roll strips

Pixelated Herringbone

FINISHED BLOCK SIZE: 16″ × 16″ ✛ **FINISHED QUILT SIZE: 64½″ × 80½″**

I love the look of a pixelated quilt, but who has the time (or patience!) to sew hundreds of 2½-inch squares together? Jelly Rolls provide a great workaround. In this project, I sew strips together lengthwise, cut them into smaller units, and then sew those pieces into a herringbone design. The result is a pixelated quilt in a fraction of the time.

Fabric Requirements

Instructions presume at least a 40″ width of fabric (WOF) after removing the selvages.

- 33 Jelly Roll strips
- 1 yard aqua fabric
- 1 yard light blue fabric
- 2¼ yards white fabric
- 5 yards backing
- 73″ × 89″ batting
- ¾ yard binding

Cutting

JELLY ROLL STRIPS

Cut 2 squares 2½″ × 2½″ from each of the 33 Jelly Roll strips, for a total of 66. Set aside. (Of these, 40 will be used in the project. The other 26 are extra.) Subcut the remnants in half to make 66 strips 2½″ × 17½+″ strips. Divide the 66 strips into 3 groups, distributing the colors equally among them:

   1 group with 12 strips
   1 group with 18 strips
   1 group with 36 strips

AQUA FABRIC

Cut 11 strips 2½″ × WOF.
   Subcut in half to make 22 strips 2½″ × 20+″.

LIGHT BLUE FABRIC

Cut 11 strips 2½″ × WOF.
   Subcut in half to make 22 strips 2½″ × 20+″.

WHITE FABRIC

Cut 30 strips 2½″ × WOF.
   Subcut in half to make 60 strips 2½″ × 20+″. Set 55 strips aside.
   Subcut the remaining 5 strips into 40 squares 2½″ × 2½″ (each strip can yield 8).

BINDING

Cut 8 strips 2½″ × WOF.

Pieced by Michelle Cain

Quilted by Ophelia Chang

Social media:
#PixelatedHerringboneQuilt

FABRICS USED
Jelly Roll: Stay Gold by Melody Miller for Ruby Star Society
Accent fabrics: Moda Bella Solids in Mediterranean and Blue Raspberry
Background fabric: Moda Bella Solids in White

Construction

All seams are a scant ¼″ unless otherwise indicated. Press the seams to 1 side as illustrated by the arrows unless instructions indicate to press open. Be sure to label all the unit pieces as they're cut. For more specifics on strip sets, see Working with Strip Sets (page 14).

Sew the Strip Sets

UNIT 1 PIECES

1 From the group of 12 Jelly Roll strips 2½″ × 17½″: Sew 2 strips together along the long edges.

2 Repeat with the remaining 10 Jelly Roll strips, for a total of 6 strip sets.

3 Press the seams of the sets to 1 side.

4 Cut the sets into 40 units 2½″ × 4½″ (each set can yield 7).

UNIT 2 PIECES

1 From the group of 18 Jelly Roll strips 2½″ × 17½″: Sew 3 strips together along the long edges.

2 Repeat with the remaining 15 Jelly Roll strips, for a total of 6 strip sets.

3 Press the seams of the sets in the same direction.

4 Cut the sets into 40 units 2½″ × 6½″ (each set can yield 7).

UNIT 3 PIECES

1 From the group of 36 Jelly Roll strips 2½″ × 17½″: Sew 3 strips together along the long edges.

2 Sew 1 aqua strip 2½″ × 20″ to 1 long side of these sewn strips. Sew 1 light blue strip 2½″ × 20″ to the other long side.

3 Repeat Steps 1–2 with the remaining 33 Jelly Roll strips, 11 aqua strips, and 11 light blue strips, for a total of 12 strip sets.

4 Press the seams of 6 strip sets toward the aqua fabric. Press the seams of the remaining 6 strip sets toward the light blue fabric.

5 Trim off the extra aqua and light blue fabric to square the sets.

6 Cut the sets into 80 units 2½″ × 10½″ (each set can yield 7).

7 Keep the Unit 3 pieces with seams pressed toward the aqua fabric separate from those with seams pressed toward the light blue fabric.

Unit 1 Pieces

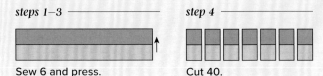

steps 1–3

Sew 6 and press.

step 4

Cut 40.

Unit 2 Pieces

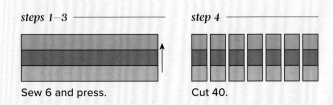

steps 1–3

Sew 6 and press.

step 4

Cut 40.

Unit 3 Pieces

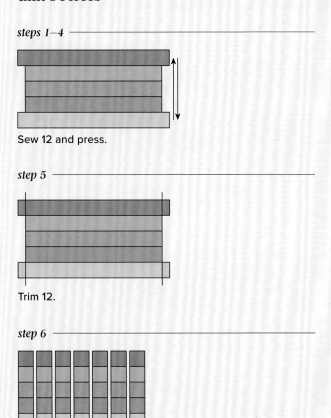

steps 1–4

Sew 12 and press.

step 5

Trim 12.

step 6

Cut 80.

PRESSING TO ONE SIDE

Unlike most of the patterns in this book, I recommend pressing all the seams in *Pixelated Herringbone* to one side. Doing so allows me to nest my seams and get accurate joins without pinning.

I made the process easier with this pattern by sewing all the Block 1s first before changing gears and sewing all the Block 2s. (My brain would have had problems toggling between the two different layouts!) I started using pins once I began sewing the completed blocks together. The bulk of the quilt top would have been cumbersome without pins at that stage.

UNIT 4 PIECES

1 Sew 3 white strips 2½″ × 20″ together along the long edges.

2 Sew 1 aqua strip 2½″ × 20″ to 1 long side of these sewn strips. Sew 1 light blue strip 2½″ × 20″ to the other long side.

3 Repeat Steps 1–2 with 27 white strips, 9 aqua strips, and 9 light blue strips, for a total of 10 strip sets.

4 Press the seams of 5 strip sets toward the aqua fabric. Press the seams of the remaining 5 strip sets toward the light blue fabric.

5 Cut the sets into 80 units 2½″ × 10½″ (each set can yield 8).

6 Keep the Unit 4 pieces with seams pressed toward the aqua fabric separate from those with seams pressed toward the light blue fabric.

UNIT 5 PIECES

1 Sew 2 white strips 2½″ × 20″ together along the long edges.

2 Repeat with 8 white strips 2½″ × 20″, for a total of 5 strip sets.

3 Press the seams of the sets to 1 side.

4 Cut the sets into 40 units 2½″ × 4½″ (each set can yield 8).

Unit 4 Pieces

steps 1–4

Sew 10 and press.

step 5

Cut 80.

Unit 5 Pieces

steps 1–3

Sew 5 and press.

step 4

Cut 40.

UNIT 6 PIECES

1 Sew 3 white strips 2½″ × 20″ together along the long edges.

2 Repeat with 12 white strips 2½″ × 20″, for a total of 5 strip sets.

3 Press the seams of the sets in the same direction.

4 Cut the sets into 40 units 2½″ × 6½″ (each set can yield 8).

Sew the Blocks

The quilt is composed of 2 different blocks. Each version contains the same pieces:

2 Unit 1 pieces

2 Unit 2 pieces

4 Unit 3 pieces

4 Unit 4 pieces

2 Unit 5 pieces

2 Unit 6 pieces

2 Jelly Roll squares 2½″ × 2½″

2 white squares 2½″ × 2½″

BLOCK 1

1 Lay out the pieces as shown in the diagram, rotating pieces to match the pressing directions indicated by the arrows whenever possible.

2 Sew each row, and press the seams as indicated.

3 Sew the rows together, and press the seams toward the top of the block.

4 Repeat Steps 1–3 to make a total of 10 blocks.

Unit 6 Pieces

steps 1–3

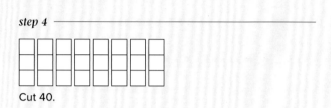

Sew 5 and press.

step 4

Cut 40.

Block 1

step 1

step 2

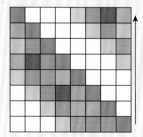

steps 3–4

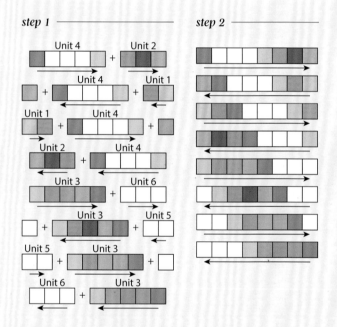

Sew 10 of Block 1 and press.

BLOCK 2

1 Lay out the pieces as shown in the diagram, rotating pieces to match the pressing directions indicated by the arrows whenever possible.

2 Sew each row, and press the seams as indicated.

3 Sew the rows together, and press the seams toward the bottom of the block.

4 Repeat Steps 1–3 to make a total of 10 blocks.

Assemble the Top

1 Lay out the blocks as illustrated in the diagram. Each of the 5 rows follows the same pattern: Block 1 + Block 2 + Block 1 + Block 2.

2 Sew each row, and press the seams open.

3 Sew the rows together, and press the seams open.

❉ *Tip* ❉

To secure the seams along the perimeter of the quilt top, take a victory lap! That is, stay stitch ¼˝ away from the edge on all 4 sides.

Finishing the Quilt

For more details on completing a quilt, see Finishing the Projects (page 108).

1 To make the backing, cut the 5 yards of backing fabric into 2 strips 89˝ × WOF. Using a ½˝ seam allowance, sew the 2 strips together along the long edges. Trim to approximately 73˝ × 89˝. Press the seam open.

2 Build the quilt sandwich: backing + batting + quilt top. Baste.

3 Quilt as desired.

4 Sew the 8 binding strips 2½˝ × WOF together, end to end, with a diagonal seam. Bind and enjoy your finished quilt!

Block 2

step 1 ——————— *step 2* ———————

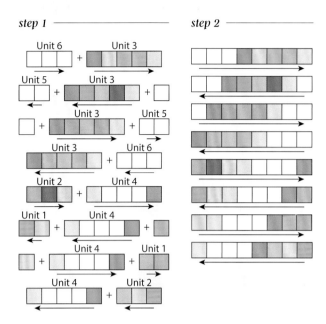

steps 3–4 ———————

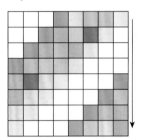

Sew 10 of Block 2 and press.

Assemble the Top

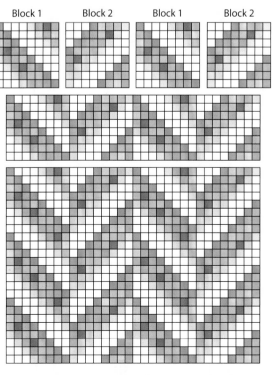

Skill Level

Lucky Medallion

FINISHED BLOCK SIZE OF THE HORSESHOE, LADYBUGS, AND CLOVERS: 12″ × 12″
FINISHED BLOCK SIZE OF THE SHOOTING STARS: 20″ × 8″ ✣ FINISHED QUILT SIZE: 80½″ × 80½″

I have a thing for ladybugs, and *Lucky Medallion* was my excuse to design my first ladybug block. You could sew two Jelly Roll strips together along the long edges and cut them into the rectangles necessary for the critters' bodies, but I recommend selecting some polka-dot yardage for the full ladybug effect.

This pattern requires more than the 40 strips available in a standard Jelly Roll, and even two full rolls may not provide the desired colors in the required quantities. I supplemented a single roll with fat quarters from the same collection as well as stashed cuts from the fabric designer's other lines.

Fabric Requirements

Instructions presume at least a 40″ width of fabric (WOF) after removing the selvages.

- 43 Jelly Roll strips
  - 1 for the horseshoe
  - 13 for the clover
  - 9 for the stars
  - 20 for the star trails*
- ⅓ yard each of 2 polka-dot fabrics for the ladybug bodies
- ⅓ yard black fabric for the ladybug accents
- 5½ yards background fabric
- 7½ yards backing
- 89″ × 89″ batting
- ¾ yard binding

** To mimic the sample's placement of colors in the star trails, use 4 strips in each of 2 colors for the outer stripes and 6 strips in each of 2 colors for the inner stripes.*

Tip

Customizing this pattern is easy. The Horseshoe, Ladybug, and Clover blocks are all 12″ squares (finished), so you could adjust the number of each that you sew or rearrange their placement in the quilt top. You could also make all your Shooting Star blocks scrappy.

Cutting

JELLY ROLL STRIPS

Horseshoe

From 1 Jelly Roll strip, cut:
- 1 rectangle 2½″ × 8½″
- 2 rectangles 2½″ × 6½″
- 2 rectangles 2½″ × 1½″
- 2 squares 1½″ × 1½″

Clover

From each of 13 Jelly Roll strips, cut:
- 5 rectangles 2½″ × 4½″
- 7 squares 2½″ × 2½″

Set aside 1 square from each strip for the stems, and then add 3 more squares to that group, for a total of 16 stem squares. Group the remaining squares, referred to as "clover squares" in the instructions, together.

Pieced by Michelle Cain

Quilted by Ophelia Chang

Social media:
#LuckyMedallionQuilt

FABRICS USED
Jelly Roll: Country Rose by Lella
Boutique for Moda
Background fabric: Moda Bella
Solids in Off-White

Stars

From each of 8 Jelly Roll strips, cut:
  2 rectangles 2½″ × 8½″
  4 squares 2½″ × 2½″ for use in the plain stars
  5 squares 2½″ × 2½″ for use in the scrappy stars
From 1 Jelly Roll strip, cut:
  8 squares 2½″ × 2½″, adding them to the squares
  for the scrappy stars cut above

Star Trails

From each of 8 Jelly Roll strips, cut:
  3 rectangles 2½″ × 12½″ for the outer stripes
From each of 12 Jelly Roll strips, cut:
  2 rectangles 2½″ × 14½″ for the inner stripes

LADYBUGS

Body Fabric

Cut 2 strips 3¾″ × WOF from each fabric for the ladybug bodies.
  Subcut the 2 strips from the 1st fabric into
  8 rectangles 3¾″ × 7½″ (each strip can yield 5).
  Subcut the 2 strips from the 2nd fabric into
  8 rectangles 3¾″ × 7½″ (each strip can yield 5).

Accent Fabric

Cut 1 strip 2″ × WOF.
  Subcut into 16 rectangles 2″ × 1½″.

<hr>

✴ *Tip* ✴

The 2″ strip will create the antenna units. Cut down a Jelly Roll strip to 2″ × WOF, and use it instead of a solid black fabric to give your ladybugs a little personality.

<hr>

Cut 4 strips 1″ × WOF.
  Subcut into 16 rectangles 1″ × 7½″ (each strip can yield 5).

BACKGROUND FABRIC

Reserve the background scraps.

Blocks

Cut 2 strips 10½″ × WOF.*
  Subcut into 4 A squares 10½″ × 10½″ (each strip can yield 3).
  * Note: If the usable fabric after removing selvages is at least 42″, cut just 1 strip.
Cut 4 strips 6½″ × WOF.
  Subcut into 64 B rectangles 6½″ × 2½″ (each strip can yield 16).
Cut 5 strips 4½″ × WOF.
  Subcut 1 strip into 1 C rectangle 4½″ × 6½″ and 2 D rectangles 4½″ × 2½″.
  Subcut 4 strips into 64 D rectangles 4½″ × 2½″ (each strip can yield 16; there will be a total of 66 D rectangles).
Cut 5 strips 3″ × WOF.
  Subcut 4 strips into 16 E rectangles 3″ × 9″ and 4 F squares 3″ × 3″ (each strip can yield 4 rectangles and 1 square).
  Subcut 1 strip into 12 F squares 3″ × 3″ (for a total of 16 F squares).
Cut 20 strips 2½″ × WOF.
  Subcut 4 strips into 12 G rectangles 2½″ × 12½″ (each strip can yield 3).
  Subcut 16 strips into 256 H squares 2½″ × 2½″ (each strip can yield 16).
Cut 5 strips 2″ × WOF.
  Subcut 3 strips into 8 J rectangles 2″ × 12½″ (each strip can yield 3).
  Subcut 2 strips into 32 K squares 2″ × 2″ (each strip can yield 20).
Cut 2 strips 1½″ × WOF.
  Subcut 1 strip into 12 L rectangles 1½″ × 3¼″.
  Subcut 1 strip into 4 L rectangles 1½″ × 3¼″ (for a total of 16 L rectangles) and 8 M rectangles 1½″ × 3″.
From the scraps, cut:
  4 H squares 2½″ × 2½″ (for a total of 260 H squares)
  2 N rectangles 2½″ × 1½″

Borders

Cut 13 strips 1½″ × WOF.

BINDING

Cut 9 strips 2½″ × WOF.

Construction

All seams are a scant ¼″ unless otherwise indicated. Press the seams open. For more specifics on the techniques used in this pattern, see Snowballing Corners (page 14) and Sewing Half-Square Triangles (page 13).

Sew the Horseshoe Block

1 Sew a horseshoe rectangle 2½″ × 1½″ and an N rectangle together along the long edges. Press. Repeat for a total of 2 units.

2 Sew a D rectangle to each of the units from Step 1 as indicated in the figure. Press.

3 Snowball the corners on a short end of the C rectangle with the 2 horseshoe squares. Trim and press.

4 Snowball the corners of the horseshoe rectangle 2½″ × 8½″ with 2 H squares as indicated in the figure. Trim and press.

5 Lay out the pieces already sewn with the additional pieces as indicated in the Horseshoe Assembly Diagram.

6 Sew the pieces into 4 rows. Press.

7 Sew the rows together. Press. The Horseshoe block will measure 12½″ × 12½″ (unfinished).

Sew the Ladybug Blocks

MAKE THE BODY UNITS

1 Sew an accent rectangle 1″ × 7½″ between 2 matching body rectangles 3¾″ × 7½″ as indicated in the figure. Press.

2 Sew an accent rectangle 1″ × 7½″ on 1 end perpendicular to the 1st accent rectangle. Press.

3 Using 2 F squares and 2 H squares, snowball the corners of the unit as indicated in the figure. Trim and press.

4 Repeat Steps 1–3 to make a total of 8 body units.

Sew the Horseshoe Block

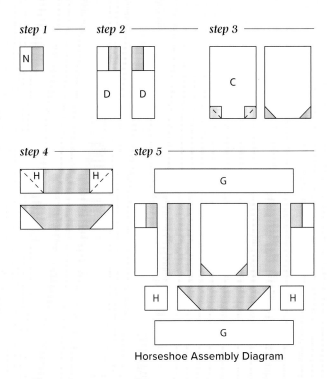

Horseshoe Assembly Diagram

Make the Body Units

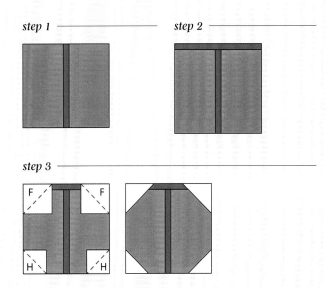

MAKE THE ANTENNA UNITS

1 Sew an accent rectangle 2″ × 1½″ to an end of an M rectangle using a diagonal seam. Trim and press.

2 Sew an accent rectangle 2″ × 1½″ to the other end of the M rectangle using a diagonal seam. Trim and press.

3 Sew an L rectangle to an end of the unit using a diagonal seam. Trim and press.

4 Sew an L rectangle to the other end of the unit using a diagonal seam. Trim and press.

5 Repeat Steps 1–4 to make a total of 8 antenna units.

ASSEMBLE THE BLOCKS

1 Sew an antenna unit onto a body as indicated in the Ladybug Assembly Diagram. Press.

2 Lay out the remaining pieces of the Ladybug block.

3 Sew the pieces in the center row together. Press.

4 Sew the rows together. Press. The Ladybug block will measure 12½″ × 12½″ (unfinished).

5 Repeat Steps 1–4 to make a total of 8 Ladybug blocks.

Sew the Clover Blocks

Each Clover block requires making 3 plain leaves and 1 leaf with a stem.

MAKE THE STEM UNITS

1 Snowball 1 corner of a stem square 2½″ × 2½″ with a K square. Trim and press.

2 Snowball the opposite corner of the same stem square with another K square. Trim and press.

3 Repeat Steps 1–2 to make a total of 16 stem units.

Make the Antenna Units

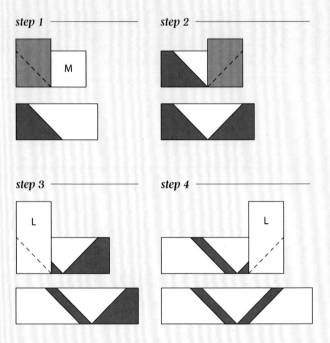

Assemble the Blocks

Ladybug Assembly Diagram

Make the Stem Units

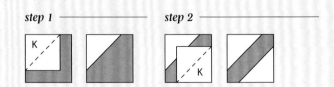

SEW THE LEAF UNITS

1 Select a clover square, a clover rectangle, and a stem unit in the same print.

2 Sew the stem unit to the clover square. Press.

3 Sew the clover rectangle and a D rectangle to the unit from Step 2 as indicated in the figure. Press.

4 Sew a B rectangle to the top of the unit as indicated in the figure. Press.

5 Repeat Steps 1–4 to make a total of 16 leaves with stems.

6 Repeat Steps 1–4 using an H square instead of a stem square, as indicated in the figure. Make a total of 48 leaf units without stems. (There will be 1 clover rectangle and multiple squares left over.)

ASSEMBLE THE BLOCKS

1 Lay out 3 leaf units and 1 leaf unit with a stem, rotating the leaves when necessary, as indicated in the Clover Assembly Diagram.

2 Sew the pieces into 2 rows. Press.

3 Sew the rows together. Press. The Clover block will measure 12½″ × 12½″ (unfinished).

4 Repeat Steps 1–3 to sew a total of 16 Clover blocks.

Sew the Shooting Stars

Plain stars use one print throughout the star. Scrappy stars use 2½″ squares in various prints to make the same shape.

PLAIN STARS

1 Select 2 star rectangles and 4 plain-star squares in the same print.

2 Snowball the ends of the rectangles with 4 H squares as indicated in the figure. Trim and press.

3 Using 2 of the plain-star squares and 2 H squares, sew 2 half-square triangles. Trim and press.

4 Lay out the pieces as indicated in the figure. (The remaining 2 plain-star squares will be sewn into the other points later.)

5 Sew the pieces into 3 columns. Press.

6 Sew the columns together. Press.

7 Repeat Steps 1–6 to make a total of 8 plain stars.

Sew the Leaf Units

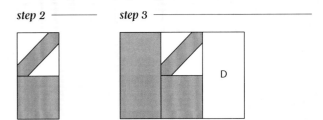

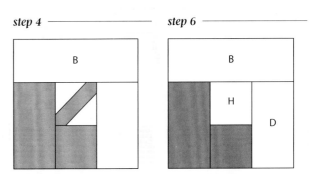

Assemble the Blocks

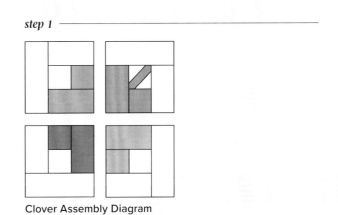

Clover Assembly Diagram

Plain Stars

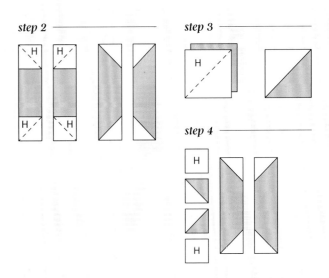

SCRAPPY STARS

1 Select 12 scrappy-star squares in a variety of prints.

2 Using 6 of the squares and 6 H squares, sew 6 half-square triangles. Trim and press.

3 Lay out the pieces as indicated in the figure. (The remaining 2 scrappy-star squares will be sewn into the other points later.)

4 Sew the pieces into 3 columns. Press.

5 Sew the columns together. Press.

6 Repeat Steps 1–5 to make a total of 4 scrappy stars.

ASSEMBLE THE SHOOTING STARS

1 Lay out a star (plain or scrappy) with 2 trail rectangles 2½″ × 12½″, 2 trail rectangles 2½″ × 14½″, 8 H squares, and the 2 star squares previously set aside, as indicated in the figure.

2 Using 6 of the H squares, snowball the ends of the trail rectangles as indicated in the Star Trail Assembly Diagram. Trim and press.

3 Using the 2 squares previously set aside, snowball the ends of the inner 2 trail rectangles as indicated in the Star Trail Assembly Diagram. (Note: If sewing a plain shooting star, ensure that the 2 squares match the adjacent star rectangle. If sewing a scrappy shooting star, the squares may or may not match the adjacent star rectangle.) Trim and press.

4 Sew the star trail pieces into rows. Press.

5 Sew the star trail rows together. Press.

6 Sew the star to the star trail section. Press. The Shooting Star block will measure 20½″ × 8½″ (unfinished).

7 Repeat Steps 1–6 to make a total of 8 plain Shooting Star blocks and 4 scrappy Shooting Star blocks.

Scrappy Stars

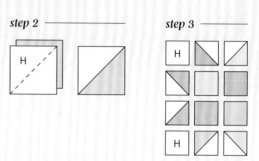

Assemble the Shooting Stars

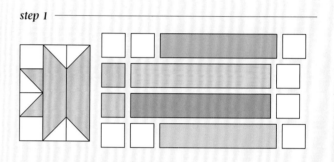

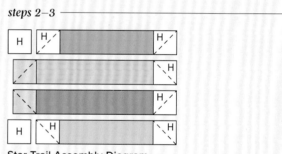

Star Trail Assembly Diagram

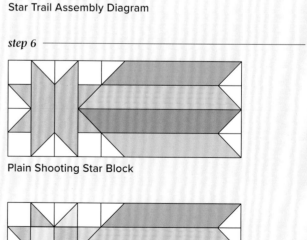

Plain Shooting Star Block

Scrappy Shooting Star Block

Assemble the Top

SEW THE CENTER GRID

1 Lay out the Horseshoe, Ladybug, and Clover blocks as indicated in the Quilt Assembly Diagram.

2 Sew the pieces into rows. Press.

3 Sew the rows together. Press.

ADD THE SHOOTING STARS

Refer to the Quilt Assembly Diagram for illustrations of the steps that follow.

1 Sew the Shooting Star blocks into 4 identical rows: 1 scrappy Shooting Star block + 1 plain Shooting Star block + 1 plain Shooting Star block. Set aside.

2 Sew the 13 background strips 1½″ × WOF together, end to end. Press the seams.

3 Cut 8 strips 60½″ from the long strip.

4 Sew a strip 1½″ × 60½″ to both long edges of each row from Step 1. Press.

5 Sew an A square to each end of 2 of the rows from Step 4. Press.

6 Sew the 2 rows without the A squares to the sides of the quilt top. Press.

7 Sew the 2 rows with the A squares to the top and bottom of the quilt top. Press.

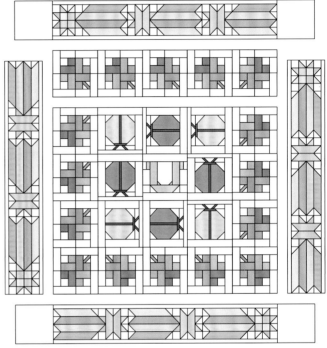

Quilt Assembly Diagram

Finishing the Quilt

For more details on completing a quilt, see Finishing the Projects (page 108).

1 To make the backing, cut the 7½ yards backing fabric into 3 strips 89″ × WOF. Using a ½″ seam allowance, sew the 3 strips together along the long edges. Press the seams open. Trim to approximately 89″ × 89″.

2 Build the quilt sandwich: backing + batting + quilt top. Baste.

3 Quilt as desired.

4 Sew the 9 binding strips 2½″ × WOF together, end to end, with a diagonal seam. Bind and enjoy your finished quilt!

BED-SIZE QUILTS

I Heart Rainbows

FINISHED BLOCK SIZE: 19″ × 14″ ❖ **FINISHED QUILT SIZE: 71½″ × 90½″**

I'll always have a place in my heart for rainbows, and this collection of them makes my inner 10-year-old particularly happy. My grown-up self is rather pleased with this quilt, too, because these colorful arcs have a simple, straightforward construction: They radiate all the joy of fabric-y rainbows without the challenges of curved piecing.

Fabric Requirements

Instructions presume at least a 40″ width of fabric (WOF) after removing the selvages.

- 38 Jelly Roll strips
    - 15 for the inner bands
    - 15 for the middle bands
    - 8 for the outer bands
- ⅝ yard fabric for the hearts
- 4½ yards background fabric
- 6¾ yards backing*
- 80″ × 99″ batting
- ¾ yard binding

* If there are 40½″ of usable fabric after removing the selvages, 5½ yards backing fabric will suffice. (See Finishing the Quilt, page 95.)

Cutting

JELLY ROLL STRIPS

Keep the cut pieces from each Jelly Roll strip together in a pile, and label the groups as an inner band, middle band, or outer band.

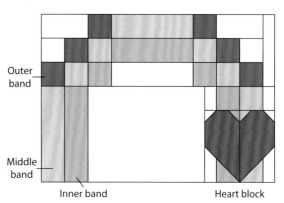

Parts of the Rainbow Block

Inner Bands

From each of 15 Jelly Roll strips for the inner bands, cut:
- 1 rectangle 2½″ × 8½″
- 1 rectangle 2½″ × 6½″
- 1 rectangle 2½″ × 3½″
- 3 squares 2½″ × 2½″
- 1 square 1½″ × 1½″

Middle Bands

From each of 15 Jelly Roll strips for the middle bands, cut:
- 1 rectangle 2½″ × 8½″
- 1 rectangle 2½″ × 6½″
- 1 rectangle 2½″ × 3½″
- 5 squares 2½″ × 2½″
- 1 square 1½″ × 1½″

Outer Bands

From each of 8 Jelly Roll strips for the outer bands, cut 12 squares 2½″ × 2½″.

Pieced by Michelle Cain
Quilted by Ophelia Chang
Social media:
#IHeartRainbowsQuilt

FABRICS USED
Jelly Roll: Rise and Shine by
Melody Miller for Ruby Star Society
Heart fabric: Moda Bella Solids in
Pomegranate
Background fabric: Moda Bella
Solids in Off-White

HEART FABRIC

Cut 5 strips 3½″ × WOF.

  Subcut into 30 rectangles 3½″ × 6½″ (each strip can yield 6).

BACKGROUND FABRIC

Blocks

Reserve the background scraps.

Cut 4 strips 8½″ × WOF.

  Subcut into 15 A rectangles 8½″ × 9½″ (each strip can yield 4).

Cut 1 strip 6½″ × WOF.

  Subcut into 15 B rectangles 6½″ × 2½″.

Cut 2 strips 4½″ × WOF.

  Subcut into 30 C rectangles 4½″ × 2½″ (each strip can yield 16).

Cut 2 strips 2½″ × WOF.

  Subcut into 30 D squares 2½″ × 2½″ (each strip can yield 16).

Cut 9 strips 1½″ × WOF.

  Subcut 3 strips into 15 E rectangles 1½″ × 6½″ (each strip can yield 6).

  Subcut 3 strips into 30 F rectangles 1½″ × 3½″ (each strip can yield 11).

  Subcut 2 strips into 30 G rectangles 1½″ × 2½″ (each strip can yield 16).

  Subcut 1 strip into 26 H squares 1½″ × 1½″.

From the scraps, cut 4 H squares 1½″ × 1½″ (for a total of 30 H squares).

Sashing

Cut 11 strips 3½″ × WOF.

Borders

Cut 8 strips 4½″ × WOF.

BINDING

Cut 9 strips 2½″ × WOF.

Construction

All seams are a scant ¼″ unless otherwise indicated. To nest seams, press to 1 side as illustrated by the arrows. In all other instances, press as desired, either open or to 1 side (those spots will not affect nesting). For more specifics on snowballing, see Snowballing Corners (page 14).

Sew the Heart Blocks

SNOWBALL THE LEFT HALF

1 Sew an F rectangle to an inner band rectangle 2½″ × 3½″. Press.

2 Place the resulting 3½″ (unfinished) square on a heart rectangle and snowball the bottom left corner, as indicated in the figure. Trim and press.

3 Using an H square and an inner band square 1½″ × 1½″ *in the same print as Step 1*, snowball the top corners, as indicated in the figure. Trim and press.

4 Repeat Steps 1–3 to make a total of 15 heart left halves.

Snowball the Left Half

step 1  step 2

step 3

SNOWBALL THE RIGHT HALF

1 Sew a middle band rectangle 2½″ × 3½″ to an F rectangle. Press.

2 Place the resulting 3½″ (unfinished) square on a heart rectangle and snowball the bottom right corner, as indicated in the figure. Trim and press.

3 Using a middle band square 1½″ × 1½″ *in the same print as Step 1* and an H square, snowball the top corners, as indicated in the figure. Trim and press.

4 Repeat Steps 1–3 to make a total of 15 heart right halves.

COMPLETE THE HEARTS

1 Sew a heart left half to a heart right half. Press to the left half.

2 Repeat to make a total of 15 hearts. Each heart block will measure 6½″ × 6½″ (unfinished).

Sew the Rainbow Blocks

1 Lay out a block as indicated in the figure, matching the inner and middle band fabrics to the ones in the heart block.

2 Sew the top 3 rows excluding the E rectangle. Press to 1 side as indicated.

3 Sew the rows together. Press.

4 Sew the E rectangle to the right side of those rows. Press the seam to the left.

5 Sew the partial row that appears above the heart. Press the seams to the right.

Snowball the Right Half

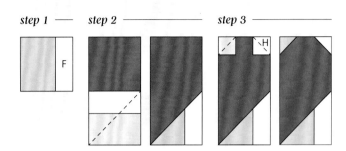

Complete the Hearts

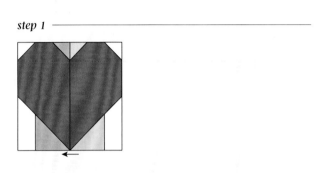

Sew the Rainbow Blocks

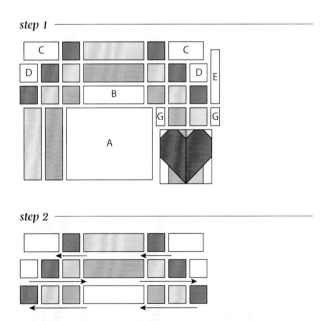

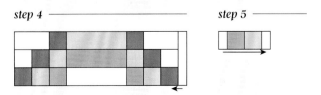

6 Sew the partial row to the heart. Press.

7 Sew the bottom row of the block. Press the 3 seams just sewn to the right.

8 Sew the top of the block to the bottom of the block. Press.

9 Repeat Steps 1–8 to make a total of 15 blocks. Each Rainbow block will measure 19½″ × 14½″ (unfinished).

Assemble the Top

For the remaining steps, refer to the Quilt Assembly Diagram.

SEW THE SASHING

1 Sew the 11 background strips 3½″ × WOF together, end to end. Press the seams.

2 From the resulting long strip, cut 10 vertical sashing rectangles 3½″ × 14½″. Set the rest aside.

3 Sew 2 vertical sashing rectangles in between 3 Rainbow blocks to create a row. Press.

4 Repeat Step 3 to make a total of 5 rows.

5 Measure each row and calculate the average length. (It should be about 63½″.)

6 Cut 4 horizontal sashing strips that length from the strip set aside in Step 2.

7 Sew the horizontal sashing strips in between the rows. Press.

ADD THE BORDERS

1 Sew the 8 background strips 4½″ × WOF together, end to end. Press the seams.

2 Measure the quilt top at 3 points (each side and the middle) to find the average length. (It should be about 82½″.)

3 Cut 2 strips that length from the long strip. Sew those strips on the sides of the quilt top. Press.

4 Measure the quilt top at 3 points (the top, bottom, and middle) to find the average width. (It should be about 71½″.)

5 Cut 2 strips that width from the long strip. Sew those strips on the top and bottom of the quilt. Press.

step 6 — step 7

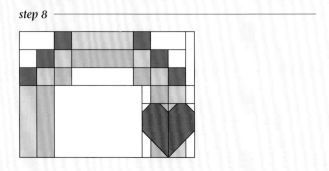

step 8

Assemble the Top

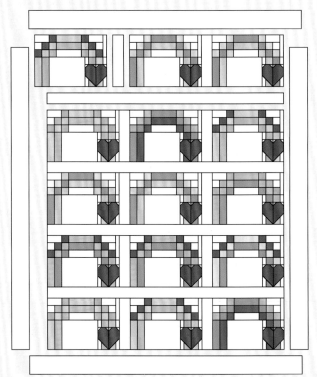

Quilt Assembly Diagram

Finishing the Quilt

For more details on completing a quilt, see Finishing the Projects (page 108).

1 To make the backing, cut the 6¾ yards backing fabric into 3 strips 80″ × WOF. Using a ½″ seam allowance, sew the 3 strips together along the long edges. Press the seams open. Trim to approximately 80″ × 99″.

(If there are 40½″ of usable fabric after removing the selvages, piece the backing with 5½ yards instead. Cut the yardage into 2 strips 99″ × WOF, and sew them together along the long edges with a ½″ seam allowance. Press the seam open. Trim to approximately 80″ × 99″.)

2 Build the quilt sandwich: backing + batting + quilt top. Baste.

3 Quilt as desired.

4 Sew the 9 binding strips 2½″ × WOF together, end to end, with a diagonal seam. Bind and enjoy your finished quilt!

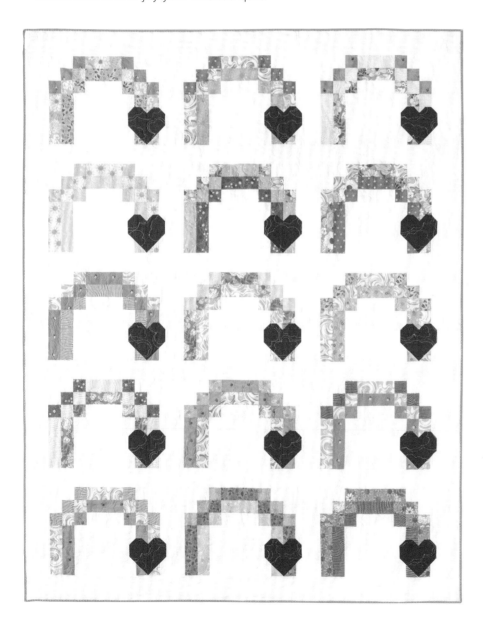

Butterfly Season

FINISHED BLOCK SIZE: 13″ × 10″ ✤ **FINISHED QUILT SIZE: 77½″ × 90½″**

Butterfly Season is another pattern that uses strip sets to facilitate piecing. To make the most of your fabric, see the sidebar Sewing Bonus Half-Square Triangles (page 99).

Fabric Requirements

Instructions presume at least a 40″ width of fabric (WOF) after removing the selvages.

- 40 Jelly Roll strips
    20 for the outer wing stripes
    20 for the middle/inner wing stripes
- ⅓ yard solid fabric for the butterfly bodies
- 6¾ yards background fabric
- 7¼ yards backing*
- 86″ × 99″ batting
- ⅞ yard binding

> ** If there are 43½″ of usable fabric after removing the selvages, 5½ yards backing fabric will suffice. (See Finishing the Quilt, page 101.)*

Cutting

JELLY ROLL STRIPS

Outer Wing Stripes
From each of 20 Jelly Roll strips, cut 2 rectangles 2½″ × 6½″ and 1 strip 2½″ × 20+″.

Middle/Inner Wing Stripes
Cut 20 Jelly Roll strips in half to make 40 strips 2½″ × 20+″.

BUTTERFLY BODIES
Cut 1 strip 5″ × WOF.

BACKGROUND FABRIC

Blocks
Cut 7 strips 6½″ × WOF.
   Subcut into 40 squares 6½″ × 6½″ (each strip can yield 6).
Cut 1 strip 4¾″.
Cut 4 strips 3½″ × WOF.
   Subcut into 40 squares 3½″ × 3½″ (each strip can yield 11).
Cut 3 strips 2½″ × WOF.
   Subcut into 40 squares 2½″ × 2½″ (each strip can yield 16).
Cut 1 strip 1¾″ × WOF.
Cut 6 strips 1½″ × WOF.
   Subcut 4 strips into 40 rectangles 1½″ × 3½″ (each strip can yield 11).
   Subcut 2 strips into 40 rectangles 1½″ × 1½″ (each strip can yield 26).

Sashing and Side Borders
Cut 15 strips 5½″ × WOF.

Top and Bottom Borders
Cut 4 strips 10½″ × WOF.

BINDING
Cut 10 strips 2½″ × WOF.

Pieced by Michelle Cain

Quilted by Ophelia Chang

Social media:
#ButterflySeasonQuilt

FABRICS USED
Jelly Roll: Beautiful Day by Corey
Yoder for Moda
Background fabric: Moda Bella
Solids in Off-White

Construction

All seams are a scant ¼″ unless otherwise indicated. Press the seams open. For more specifics on the techniques used in this pattern, see Sewing Half-Square Triangles (page 13), Snowballing Corners (page 14), and Working with Strip Sets (page 14).

To work with fabrics that have a clear directionality to their design, see the sidebar Using Directional Fabrics (below).

USING DIRECTIONAL FABRICS

If any of the Jelly Roll strips you're using have a directional design that you want to maintain as you sew, you'll need to piece the wings individually. Instead of following the instructions under Sew the Strip Sets for the Wings (below), sew your wings with this process:

1 Gather 3 strips 2½″ × 20″: 1 for the outer stripe, 1 for the middle stripe, and 1 for the inner stripe. (Keep the 2 corresponding outer stripe rectangles 2½″ × 6½″ on hand.)

2 From each of the 3 strips, cut 2 rectangles 2½″ × 6½″ and 2 rectangles 2½″ × 3½″.

3 Lay out the rectangles in the configurations indicated in the figure. In this example, the rust fabric is the outer stripe, and the inner stripe is a directional fabric. All the green pieces are oriented accordingly, ensuring that the smiley faces will be upright in the final block.

4 Sew each set of 3, and press the seams.

5 Pick up with Step 1 under Sew the Wing Tops (page 99).

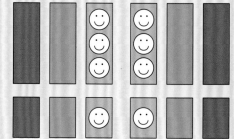

Sew the Strip Sets for the Wings

1 Sew a middle stripe strip in between an inner stripe strip and an outer stripe strip. Press.

2 Cut the strip set into 2 squares 6½″ × 6½″ and 2 rectangles 6½″ × 3½″. Press.

3 Repeat Step 1 to make a total of 20 strip sets for the wings and then, following Step 2, cut each set into the required 2 squares and 2 rectangles.

Sew the Strip Sets for the Wings

step 1

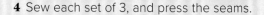

step 2

Sew the Wing Tops

1 Lay out the wing tops 6½″ × 6½″ and the wing bottoms 6½″ × 3½″ as indicated in the figure. (The outer stripes are rust in the figure.) Gather the 2 rectangles 2½″ × 6½″ that are the same fabric as the outer stripe.

2 Using 2 background squares 6½″ × 6½″, make 2 half-square triangles with the wing tops as indicated in the figure. Trim and press.

3 Sew an outer stripe rectangle 2½″ × 6½″ to the bottom of each wing top. Press.

4 Trim the height of the rectangles just added to 1¼″ as indicated in the figure.

5 Snowball the outer bottom corner of each unit with a background square 1½″ × 1½″. Trim and press. The size of each wing top is 6½″ × 7½″ (unfinished).

6 Repeat Steps 1–5 to make a total of 20 pairs of wing tops.

Sew the Wing Tops

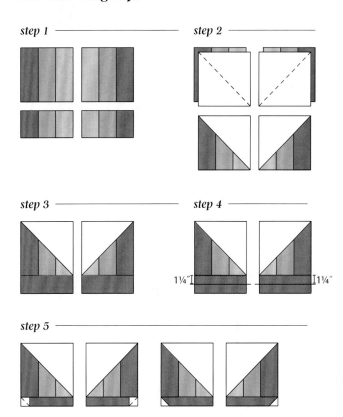

step 1

step 2

step 3

step 4

1¼″   1¼″

step 5

SEWING BONUS HALF-SQUARE TRIANGLES

Snowballing the butterfly wings in this project creates some waste. Perhaps you can see yourself using the triangular cut-offs in future scrappy projects. I didn't think I would sew with scraps of that size and shape, so I sewed the would-be cut-offs into half-square triangles (HSTs) as I sewed the pattern.

The figures that follow show my step-by-step process with a square 6½″ × 6½″.

1 First, I followed the basic block instructions and marked a diagonal line from 1 corner to the opposite corner.

2 Then, straying from the basic instructions, I marked a 2nd diagonal line ½″ from the original line.

3 I sewed along both lines, and cut between the 2 seams.

4 The resulting pieces look like the figures below, 1 that I used in a Butterfly block and 1 that is a bonus HST.

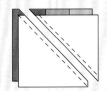

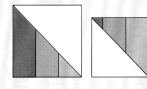

Sew the Wing Bottoms

1 Trim the width of the outer stripes of the 2 wing bottoms to 1¼″ as indicated in the figure.

2 Snowball the inner bottom corners of the 2 wing bottoms with background squares 3½″ × 3½″. Trim and press.

3 Snowball the outer bottom corners of the 2 wing bottoms with background squares 2½″ × 2½″. Trim and press.

4 Add a background rectangle 1½″ × 3½″ to the outer edge of both units. Press. The size of each wing bottom is 6½″ × 3½″ (unfinished).

5 Repeat Steps 1–4 to make a total of 20 pairs of wing bottoms.

Sew the Strip Sets for the Body Units

1 Sew the background strip 4¾″ × WOF to a long edge of the body strip 5″ × WOF. Press. Sew the background strip 1¾″ × WOF to the other long edge of the body strip. Press.

2 Cut the strip set into 20 body units 1½″ × 10½″.

Assemble the Butterfly Blocks

1 Lay out 4 wing units with a body unit as indicated in the figure.

2 Sew the wing tops to the wing bottoms. Press.

3 Sew the wings to the body unit. Press. The block size is 13½″ × 10½″ (unfinished).

4 Repeat Steps 1–3 to make 20 Butterfly blocks.

Assemble the Top

For the remaining steps, refer to the Quilt Assembly Diagram, page 101.

SEW THE SASHING AND SIDE BORDERS

1 Sew the 15 sashing/border strips 5½″ × WOF together, end to end. Press the seams.

2 From the resulting long strip, cut 15 vertical sashing rectangles 5½″ × 10½″. Set the rest aside.

3 Sew 3 vertical sashing rectangles in between 4 Butterfly blocks to create 1 row. Press.

4 Repeat Step 3 to sew 5 rows.

5 Measure each row and calculate the average length. (It should be about 67½″.)

6 Cut 4 horizontal sashing strips that length from the strip set aside in Step 2.

7 Sew the horizontal sashing strips in between the rows. Press.

Sew the Wing Bottoms

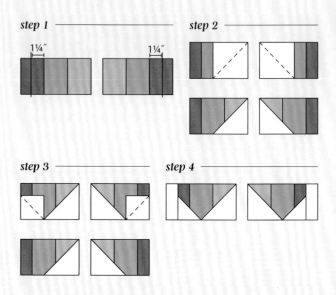

step 1   1¼″   1¼″   *step 2*

step 3   *step 4*

Sew the Strip Sets for the Body Units

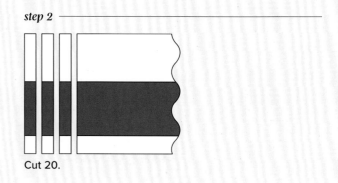

step 2

Cut 20.

Assemble the Butterfly Blocks

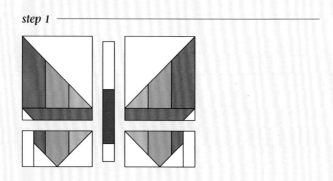

step 1

8 Measure the quilt top at 3 points (each side and the middle) to find the average length. (It should be about 70½".) Cut 2 side border strips that length from the remaining long strip.

9 Sew the side borders on the sides of the quilt. Press.

ADD THE TOP AND BOTTOM BORDERS

1 Sew the 4 background strips 10½" × WOF together, end to end. Press the seams.

2 Measure the quilt top at 3 points (the top, bottom, and middle) to find the average width. (It should be about 77½".)

3 Cut 2 strips that width from the long strip. Sew those strips on the top and bottom of the quilt top. Press.

Finishing the Quilt

For more details on completing a quilt, see Finishing the Projects (page 108).

1 To make the backing, cut the 7¼ yards backing fabric into 3 strips 86" × WOF. Using a ½" seam allowance, sew the 3 strips together along the long edges. Press the seams open. Trim to approximately 86" × 99".

(If there are 43½" of usable fabric after removing the selvages, piece the backing with 5½ yards backing fabric. Cut the yardage into 2 strips 99" × WOF, and sew them together along the long edges with a ½" seam. Press the seam open. Trim to approximately 86" × 99".)

2 Build the quilt sandwich: backing + batting + quilt top. Baste.

3 Quilt as desired.

4 Sew the 10 binding strips 2½" × WOF together, end to end, with a diagonal seam. Bind and enjoy your finished quilt!

Quilt Assembly Diagram

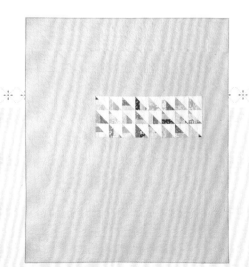

I made bonus half-square triangles when sewing the wing tops. You could sew these bonus blocks into a coordinating pillow or a baby quilt. I placed some of mine on the back of my quilt.

All the Xs

FINISHED BLOCK SIZE: 18″ × 18″ ⊕ **FINISHED QUILT SIZE: 102½″ × 102½″**

All the Xs makes the most of a single Jelly Roll to create a generously sized bed quilt. The sample's gray background allowed me to use all 40 strips without editing anything out. In fact, I'd argue that the low volumes shine here and add needed variety to the many medium and dark tones found in the fabric collection.

Fabric Requirements

Please note: Instructions presume at least a 41″ width of fabric (WOF) after removing the selvages.

- 40 Jelly Roll strips
    - 32 for the outer Xs
    - 8 for the inner Xs
- ¾ yard solid fabric for the accent Xs
- 7¾ yards background fabric
- 9¼ yards backing
- 111″ × 111″ batting
- 1 yard binding

✳ *Tip* ✳

This is the biggest quilt in the book. If you're going to splurge on wideback yardage or longarming services, this is the project to do it with!

Cutting

JELLY ROLL STRIPS

Outer Xs
From each of 32 Jelly Roll strips, cut:
  2 rectangles 2½″ × 6½″
  4 rectangles 2½″ × 4½″
  4 squares 2½″ × 2½″

Inner Xs
From each of 8 Jelly Roll strips, cut:
  2 rectangles 2½″ × 10½″, reserving the
   8 remnants 2½″ × 20″

ACCENT X BLOCKS

Cut 1 strip 10½″ × WOF.
  Subcut into 1 strip 10½″ × 20½″ and 2 strips 4½″ × 20½″ as indicated in the figure.

Cut 1 strip 2½″ × WOF.
  Subcut into 1 rectangle 2½″ × 10½″ and 2 rectangles 2½″ × 4½″.

Pieced by Michelle Cain
Quilted by Ophelia Chang
Social media:
#AllTheXsQuilt

FABRICS USED
Jelly Roll: Strawberry Lemonade
by Sherri and Chelsi for Moda
Accent fabric: Moda Bella Solids in
Dark Teal
Background fabric: Moda Bella
Solids in Gray

BACKGROUND FABRIC

Reserve the background scraps.

⁜ *Tip* ⁜

Further cutting the A and B squares later during construction will result in bias edges. If you're a fan of starching fabric, it's worth taking the extra time to starch and press now, before cutting into the background yardage.

Cut 1 strip 27¼″ × WOF.
  Subcut 1 A square 26¾″ × 26¾″ and 2 B squares 13⅝″ × 13⅝″ as indicated in the figure.

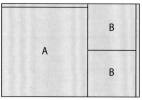

Cut 2 strips 26¾″ × WOF.
  Subcut each strip into 1 A square 26¾″ × 26¾″ and 3 C squares 8½″ × 8½″ as indicated in the figure.
  (In total, there will be 3 A squares.)

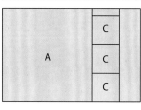

Cut 8 strips 8½″ × WOF.
  Subcut into 30 C squares 8½″ × 8½″ (each strip can yield 4; there will be a total of 36 C squares).
Cut 4 strips 6½″ × WOF.
  Subcut into 64 D rectangles 6½″ × 2½″ (each strip can yield 16).
Cut 9 strips 4½″ × WOF.
  Subcut 2 strips in half to make 4 E strips 4½″ × 20½″.
  Subcut 7 strips into 63 F squares 4½″ × 4½″ (each strip can yield 9).
Cut 12 strips 2½″ × WOF.
  Subcut 8 strips in half to make 16 G strips 2½″ × 20½″.
  Subcut 4 strips into 64 H squares 2½″ × 2½″ (each strip can yield 16).
From the scraps, cut:
  1 F square 4½″ × 4½″ (for a total of 64 F squares)
  4 J rectangles 2½″ × 4½″

BINDING

Cut 12 strips 2½″ × WOF.

Construction

All seams are a scant ¼″ unless otherwise indicated. Press the seams open. For more specifics on the techniques used in this pattern, see Sewing Half-Square Triangles (page 13) and Working with Strip Sets (page 14).

⁜ *Tip* ⁜

I recommend using pins for constructing this pattern's big blocks. Doing so will result in more precise piecing. Because I pin liberally throughout these instructions, I do not bother with pressing any seams to the side.

Sew the Outer X Arms

1 Sew an outer X rectangle 2½″ × 6½″ to a D rectangle along the long edges. Press.

2 Repeat with the remaining outer X rectangles 2½″ × 6½″ and D rectangles for a total of 64 units.

3 Select 2 outer X rectangles 2½″ × 4½″ and a unit from Step 2, all in the same print. Sew the 2 outer X rectangles to either end of the unit. Press.

4 Repeat with the remaining outer X rectangles 2½″ × 4½″ and units from Step 2, for a total of 64 outer X arms.

Sew the Outer X Arms

step 1 ─────────────

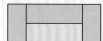

step 3 ─────────────

Sew the Outer X Half-Square Triangles

1 Using 8 Jelly Roll squares (4 each of 2 different prints), make 4 half-square triangles (HSTs). Trim and press.

2 Repeat with the remaining Jelly Roll squares, for a total of 16 sets of 4 HSTs.

3 Taking 1 set at a time, add an H square to each HST in the configuration indicated in the figure. Press.

Sew the Inner X Strip Sets

1 Sew a G strip to both long edges of an inner X remnant 2½″ × 20″. Press, and trim to square the set.

2 Repeat for a total of 8 strip sets.

3 Cut each strip set into 4 units 6½″ × 4½″, for a total of 32 inner X arms.

Sew the Outer X Half-Square Triangles

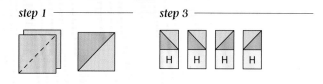

Sew the Inner X Strip Sets

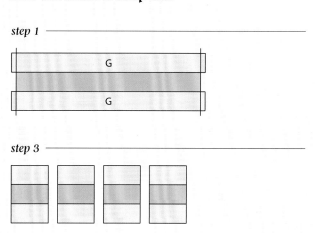

KEEPING EVERYTHING CENTERED

This pattern requires working with some large, long pieces. To ensure that the smaller arms of the Xs are centered in the finished blocks, match up the midpoints of the units you're sewing. To do so, follow these simple steps:

1 Fold the pieces you're sewing together in half lengthwise, and finger-press the midpoint of each.

2 Lay one on top of the other, right sides together, and match the creases. Pin the midpoint intersection. Pin along the rest of the seam.

3 Sew the seam, and press.

4 Finish sewing the block, ensuring that the midpoints of the remaining pieces match up.

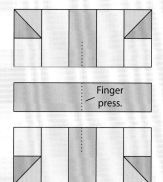

Finger press.

Assemble the Main X Blocks

See the accompanying sidebar Keeping Everything Centered, page 105.

1 Lay out the pieces with an inner X rectangle 2½″ × 10½″ as indicated in the figure. Note the orientation of the HSTs.

2 Sew the top and bottom rows. Press.

3 Sew the rows together. Press.

4 Lay out the remaining pieces, including 4 F squares, around that unit. Be sure to match the prints in the outer X arms to the prints in the HSTs.

5 Sew each of the rows. Press.

6 Sew the rows together. Press.

7 Repeat Steps 1–6 for a total of 16 Main X blocks. Each Main X block will measure 18½″ × 18½″ (unfinished).

Sew the Accent X Strip Sets

1 Sew 1 E strip to the long side of an accent X strip 4½″ × 20½″. Press. Repeat with another E strip and the remaining accent X strip 4½″ × 20½″. Cut both strip sets into 8 units 2½″ × 8½″, for a total of 16 units.

2 Sew 2 E strips to the long sides of the accent X strip 10½″ × 20½″. Press. Cut the strip set into 8 units 2½″ × 18½″.

Assemble the Accent X Blocks

To piece more efficiently, 8 of the 9 Accent X blocks use units from the strip sets. (The 9th block is pieced individually.)

1 Sew a J rectangle on an end of 2 accent X rectangles 2½″ × 4½″. Press. Combined with the units from the strip sets, there will be 18 units 2½″ × 8½″.

2 Sew a J rectangle on either end of the accent X rectangle 2½″ × 10½″. Press. Combined with the units from the strips set, there will be 9 units 2½″ × 18½″.

3 Lay out the pieces for 1 block, including 4 C squares, as indicated in the figure.

4 Sew the top and bottom rows. Press.

5 Sew the rows together. Press.

6 Repeat Steps 3–5 for a total of 9 Accent X blocks. Each Accent X block will measure 18½″ × 18½″ (unfinished).

Assemble the Main X Blocks

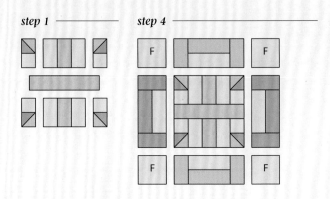

step 1   step 4

Sew the Accent X Strip Sets

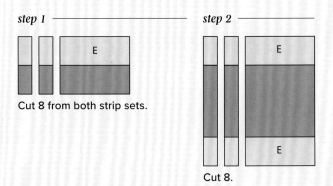

step 1

Cut 8 from both strip sets.

step 2

E

E

Cut 8.

Assemble the Accent X Blocks

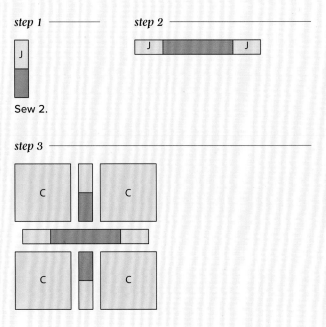

step 1

J

Sew 2.

step 2

J   J

step 3

C   C

C   C

Tip

These diagonal cuts will create bias edges. Take care in handling these pieces and the quilt top once it's completed to avoid distorting the fabric.

Assemble the Top

1 Cut the 3 A squares diagonally into quarters to make 12 setting triangles.

2 Cut the 2 B squares diagonally into halves to make 4 corner triangles.

3 Lay out the blocks as indicated in the Quilt Assembly Diagram.

4 Sew the blocks into rows. Press.

5 Sew the rows together. Press.

6 Square up the quilt top if necessary.

Finishing the Quilt

For more details on completing a quilt, see Finishing the Projects (page 108).

1 To make the backing, cut the 9¼ yards backing fabric into 3 strips 111″ × WOF. Using a ½″ seam allowance, sew the 3 strips together along the long edges. Press the seams open. Trim to approximately 111″ × 111″.

2 Build the quilt sandwich: backing + batting + quilt top. Baste.

3 Quilt as desired.

4 Sew the 12 binding strips 2½″ × WOF together, end to end, with a diagonal seam. Bind and enjoy your finished quilt!

Assemble the Top

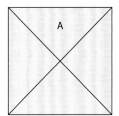

step 1 A

step 2 B

step 3

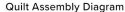

Quilt Assembly Diagram

FINISHING THE PROJECTS

Even if you have a preferred finishing process, it's always nice to step inside other quilters' shoes and see how they tackle the steps of quilting and binding a project. The specifics of my own process are detailed here.

Deciding on the Quilting Plan

I am a straight-line quilter who occasionally ventures into free-motion quilting. If a particular project, such as *Neighborly* (page 16), would benefit from straight lines, I'll likely quilt it myself on my domestic machine. If the project is a bed-size quilt or if the design merits something curvy or something more elaborate than I can accomplish with my walking foot, I will hand it off to a longarmer.

If you choose to go that second route, I recommend having a conversation with any new-to-you longarmers. The fabric requirements for the quilt backs in this book include 8 inches of overage in both width and length to accommodate longarming services, but some longarmers may have additional requirements for preparing a quilt top. It's best to know that information before you piece a backing.

Building and Basting the Quilt Sandwich

I spray-baste the projects I quilt on my domestic. You may choose to baste with pins or thread, but I know that, for me, the fastest way to a finish is to use an adhesive like Odif 505 Spray. I like to baste on my hardwood floor, using the slats to help me keep the backing and quilt top straight.

I use painter's tape to adhere the backing to the floor and then spray one side of the batting before setting the sticky side over the backing and smoothing it out. Then I spray the untreated side of the batting, lay the quilt top over it, and smooth that out. After spray basting, I set the adhesive by ironing both sides of the quilt sandwich.

Binding Your Project

All the projects in this collection use 2½-inch width-of-fabric strips to bind. You may opt to use 2½-inch strips cut on the bias. Keep in mind, however, that bias strips will likely require more fabric than indicated in the instructions.

Making the Binding

To make binding, lay a strip perpendicular to another, right sides together. Sew the strips together with a diagonal seam, as illustrated below.

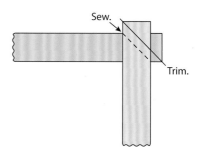

Trim the seam allowance to ¼ inch, and press the seam open.

Continue this process until all the binding strips have been sewn together and all the seams have been trimmed and pressed. Then fold the resulting long strip in half along the entire length, matching the wrong sides, and press.

Attaching the Binding

After quilting, trim the excess batting and backing off the quilt sandwich. To attach the binding, start in the middle of a side of the quilt, aligning the raw edges of the binding with the raw edges of the quilt sandwich, and leave a tail of several inches. (If I plan on hand-finishing the binding, I usually attach the binding to the front of the quilt. If I plan on machine-finishing the binding, I'll usually attach it to the back.)

Install your walking foot, and start sewing a ¼-inch seam along the first edge. Stop sewing ¼ inch before the first corner, as illustrated below, and take your quilt off the machine.

Fold the binding away from the quilt.

Then make a second fold, bringing the binding back onto the quilt sandwich and aligning its raw edges to the quilt's raw edges. Use a clip to keep the folded corner in place.

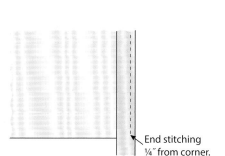

End stitching ¼″ from corner.

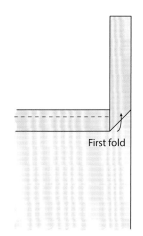

First fold

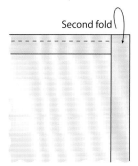

Second fold

Start quilting again ¼ inch from the corner. Continue attaching the binding to the project, and stop about 12 inches or so from where you began. Lay the beginning tail and ending tail over each other, and trim them so that there is 2½ inches of overlap. Open up each tail, match their right sides together, and sew them together with a diagonal seam. Trim the seam and press it open. Finish sewing the binding to the quilt.

Fold the binding to the opposite side of the quilt, and finish it—by hand or by machine—as desired.

Preparing to Hang a Project

I find the easiest way to add hangers for a wall hanging, such as *Neighborly* (page 16), is by adding fabric triangles to the top corners before binding. To do this, cut 2 squares of fabric—5-inch squares will do the trick. Fold them in half diagonally, and press. As indicated in the figure on the right, place the triangles in the top corners of the back of the quilt, aligning the raw edges of the triangles with the raw edges of the quilt sandwich. Machine-baste the triangles about ⅛″ from the edge, and then bind as usual. To hang, cut a dowel rod to slide snuggly in the pockets created by the triangles.

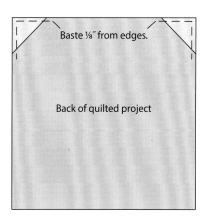

Baste ⅛″ from edges.

Back of quilted project

TEMPLATES

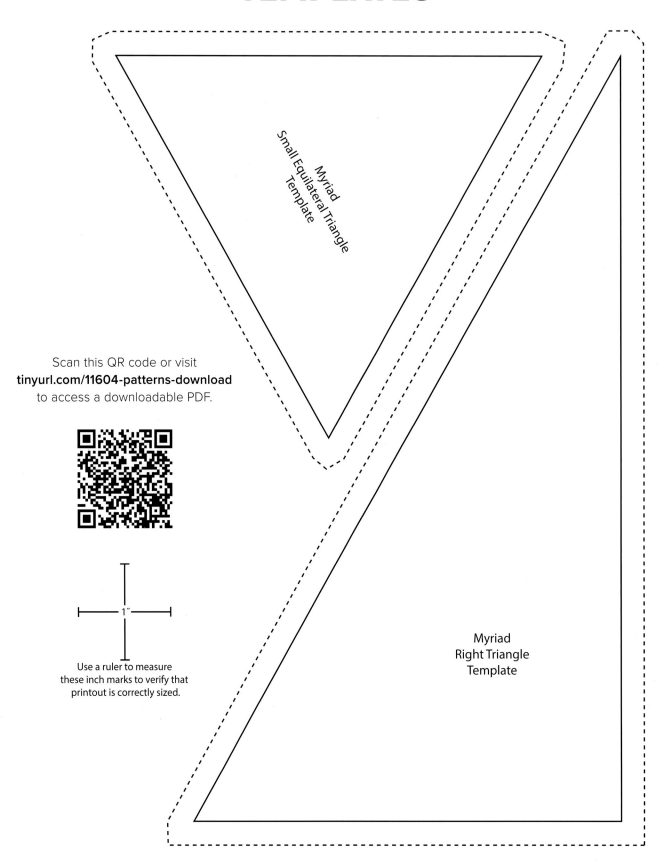

Myriad
Small Equilateral Triangle
Template

Scan this QR code or visit
tinyurl.com/11604-patterns-download
to access a downloadable PDF.

1″

Use a ruler to measure
these inch marks to verify that
printout is correctly sized.

Myriad
Right Triangle
Template

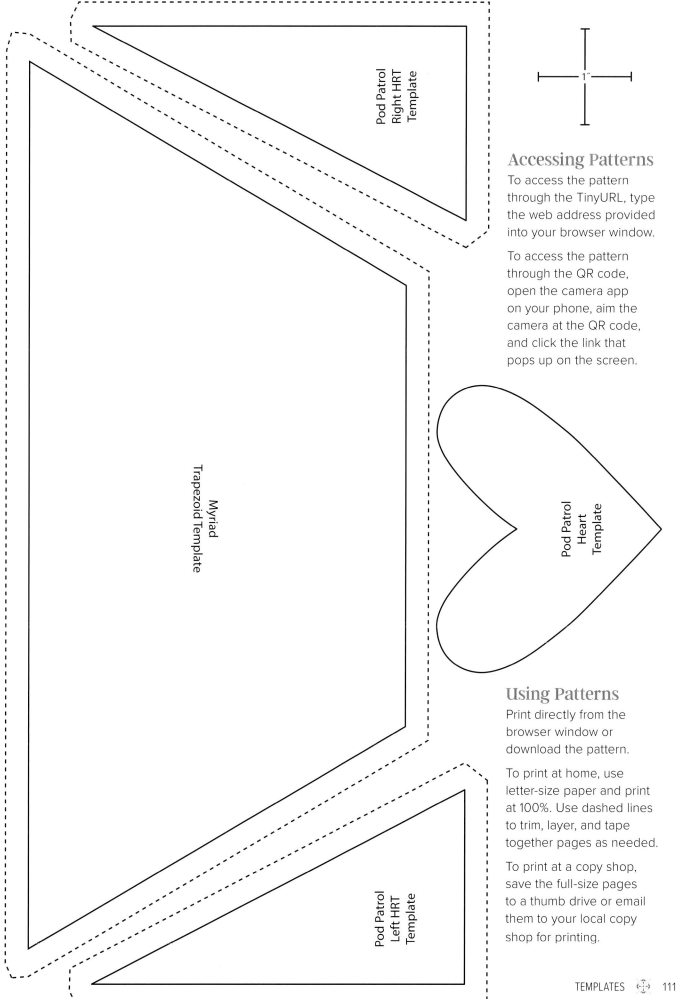

Pod Patrol
Right HRT
Template

1″

Accessing Patterns

To access the pattern through the TinyURL, type the web address provided into your browser window.

To access the pattern through the QR code, open the camera app on your phone, aim the camera at the QR code, and click the link that pops up on the screen.

Myriad
Trapezoid Template

Pod Patrol
Heart
Template

Using Patterns

Print directly from the browser window or download the pattern.

To print at home, use letter-size paper and print at 100%. Use dashed lines to trim, layer, and tape together pages as needed.

To print at a copy shop, save the full-size pages to a thumb drive or email them to your local copy shop for printing.

Pod Patrol
Left HRT
Template

ABOUT THE AUTHOR

Michelle Lander Cain tried rather hard not to become a quilter. After growing up outside of Lancaster County, Pennsylvania, and having a mom who began quilting in the 1990s, this was a formidable challenge. A chance encounter with Denyse Schmidt's work, however, introduced Michelle to the world of modern quilting and convinced her there might be a place for her in it. She made her first quilt in 2013 and hasn't looked back.

Wanting to connect with other makers, Michelle became active in the New Hampshire Modern Quilt Guild and started blogging about her quilting adventures as From Bolt to Beauty in 2014. In 2020, she formally launched From Bolt to Beauty patterns. Her projects have been featured at QuiltCon and in magazines like *Curated Quilts* and *Love Patchwork & Quilting*.

Photo by Kathryn Costello

In a previous life, Michelle wrote marketing copy and edited books, magazines, and websites. This book, her first, combines her past professional experience with her current creative obsession, and she had a blast writing it!

Michelle and her husband, Brad, live in Massachusetts with their two teenage sons and two naughty Golden Retrievers.

To see Michelle's other work, visit her website: **FromBoltToBeauty.com** or Instagram feed **@FromBoltToBeauty**